From Citrus to Limoncello

History, Secrets, and Recipes of the Coast

Alessandro Buonocore

2023 © Alessandro Buonocore

All rights reserved

I want to express profound gratitude to my wife, Francesca, who, with her love for homemade limoncello, ignited the spark of inspiration for this book.

Alessandro

SUMMARY

INTRODUCTION 1
TRACKING LIMONCELLO: HISTORY, MYTHS, AND
REALITIES 3
SCENTS OF THE COAST: THE LEMON AS CULTURAL AND
CULINARY ICON 7
SECRET RECIPE FOR THE PERFECT LIMONCELLO 12
LIMONCELLO IN THE KITCHEN: EXCEPTIONAL DISHES
FOR EVERY OCCASION 25
LIMONCELLO MIXOLOGY: COCKTAILS AND APERITIFS
FROM THE SORRENTO AND AMALFI COAST 30
FIRST COURSES AROMATIZED: THE DELIGHTS OF
LIMONCELLO IN THE KITCHEN 44
EXCELLENCE MAIN COURSES: LIMONCELLO ON THE
TABLE 61
LIMONCELLO DESSERTS: A TOUCH OF SWEETNESS FROM
THE AMALFI COAST 78
CONCLUSIONS 92

INTRODUCTION

Welcome to a culinary journey through Mediterranean cuisine, where the fresh and vibrant flavor of limoncello combines with delightful ingredients to create a symphony of tastes that will delight your senses. This book will take you on a fascinating journey through the history, culture, and cuisine of Italy, all encapsulated in a bottle of lemon liqueur.

Limoncello is much more than a mere liqueur; it is a symbol of Italian hospitality, the joy of living, and a passion for fresh, high-quality ingredients. This golden and fragrant beverage was born under the radiant sun of the Sorrento and Amalfi coasts, amidst lush lemon groves that embrace the Tyrrhenian Sea. Its history is steeped in legends and traditions passed down from generation to generation.

Throughout this book, we will explore the origins of Limoncello, its evolution over time, and guide you through its homemade production. We will introduce you to fascinating stories related to this beverage and, most importantly, delight you with a variety of recipes that feature Limoncello as the main ingredient.

Once you have crafted your homemade limoncello, we will use it to prepare a series of recipes inspired by this extraordinary liqueur. You will discover how limoncello can transform fish, meat, and pasta dishes into unique culinary experiences, adding a citrusy and refreshing note.

We will guide you through a series of main courses that will tantalize your palate, and for those seeking a refreshing sip, we have also prepared a selection of limoncello cocktails.

Whether you are a lover of traditional Italian cuisine or a culinary adventurer, you will find a recipe in this book to satisfy your desires. We hope this book inspires you to discover, savor, and celebrate this Italian wonder. It's time to embark on this journey into the world of Limoncello, where tradition merges with creativity, and flavor is a hymn to life.

Welcome aboard!

TRACKING LIMONCELLO: HISTORY, MYTHS, AND REALITIES

The roots of Limoncello run deep in the history of the Naples Coasts, an area of extraordinary beauty and rich in history. This stretch of coastline extends for over 50 kilometers, from Sorrento to Positano, Vietri sul Mare, embracing more than 15 municipalities. It is a place of great historical significance, having been the heart of one of the Maritime Republics since

839 A.D. In addition, it has been recognized as a UNESCO World Heritage site, a testament to its cultural and natural importance.

Limoncello, however, is a treasure of this region that emerged only in the early 20th century. The most credible legend suggests that its story began in a picturesque inn on the Azure Island of Capri. The owner, Maria Antonietta, tended to a lush garden of lemons and oranges and would offer her homemade liqueur to the guests of her inn. Guests were enthralled by it, and it seems that even Axel Munthe, one of the fathers of modern psychiatry, was a regular patron of the inn and a lover of the drink. Axel, along with his intellectual friends on the island, would often visit Maria Antonietta's inn after lunch to enjoy this beverage as a digestif. Later, the heirs of the lady had the insight to start small-scale production of Limoncello following the family recipe. In fact, the name Limoncello was registered and patented in Capri in 1988 by Massimo Canale, Maria Antonietta's nephew, who, among the fragrant trees, opened a small restaurant after World War II. The restaurant became known for a specialty: a lemon liqueur prepared according to the ancient recipe passed down by his grandmother. Word of mouth and the fame of this creation spread rapidly.

However, the exact origin of Limoncello remains shrouded in mystery, with numerous legends and stories claiming its creation. The Amalfi and Sorrento coasts, famous for lemon production, are the backdrop for these fascinating narratives.

For example, in the coastal region, the story goes that it was Zeus himself who gave the recipe for this delicious beverage to an inhabitant of the land of the sirens. In Amalfi, some even claim that the liqueur has very ancient origins, almost linked to lemon cultivation. However, as often happens in these circumstances, the truth is cloudy, and there are many suggestive hypotheses. Some believe that Limoncello was used by fishermen and farmers in the morning to combat the cold, even at the time of the Saracen invasion. Others, on the other hand, believe that the recipe was born within a monastic convent to delight the monks between one prayer and another.

The truth, perhaps, we will never know. But beyond purely regional matters, the traditional yellow liqueur has crossed borders for decades, conquering markets all over the world. Bottles of Limoncello are found on the shelves of overseas markets, and new significant commercial scenarios are developing in Asian markets. Limoncello, therefore, truly risks becoming a globally renowned product on par with Bitter or Amaretto.

The evolution of Limoncello over time is a story of success and expansion. What began as a hidden treasure of the Coast gradually transformed into a beloved product worldwide. In the 1980s and 1990s, Limoncello began to gain international popularity thanks to tourists who returned home with a bottle of this fragrant and golden beverage. The growing demand led to commercial-scale production and the emergence of numerous brands on the market. Limoncello was now an ambassador of Italian culture, carrying with it the scent of lemons and the atmosphere of the Sorrento and Amalfi Coasts worldwide.

TRADITIONAL PRODUCTION

The lemons used for Limoncello are primarily of the "Sfusato" variety, grown on an area of 700 hectares of lemon groves by approximately 1,500 vineyard owners. This lemon is distinguished by its elongated shape and smooth citron-yellow peel. It is a fruit characterized by intense aroma and fragrance, abundant and highly acidic juice, and a lively pale yellow color.

Every detail of production pays homage to tradition, from the chestnut pole trellises at varying heights to protecting the plants during cold periods. In every cultivated hectare, there are over 800 lemon trees, with a maximum production capacity of 35 tons of lemons. These lemons are the secret ingredient that makes the Limoncello of the Coast unique. To protect this tradition and the product's quality, the Sorrento and Amalfi Coast Lemon has been recognized with the Protected Geographical Indication (PGI) designation, ensuring that it is produced according to traditional criteria in one of the municipalities in the territory, ranging from Vico Equense to Massa Lubrense and the island of Capri.

Imagine a landscape where the intense yellow of lemons blends with the green of vegetation and the deep blue of the sea. Here, the gentle breeze blowing from the sea cradles the lemon tree leaves and refreshes the diligent hands of those devoted to this ancient tradition. The Coast's lemon is much more than a simple fruit; it becomes a symbol of Sorrento, Amalfi, and, in general, the entire Coast. It encapsulates the captivating and fascinating stories of enchanted travelers. This fruit holds the wisdom of local gardeners and the tenacity of a community building its future through daily hard work. Tenacity is the word that comes to mind when observing the surrounding landscape. A landscape that the locals often take for granted but fascinates visitors with its extraordinary structure. The coastal terraces resemble green stairs gently descending toward the sea, a unique form of cultivation that has allowed generations to feed and thrive. These gardens carved into the mountains are the result of human determination, stone by stone, with sweat and hope for a better future. They symbolize human strength that has transformed the mountains into magnificent hanging gardens. The construction of the terraces requires sophisticated building skills, accumulated through centuries of experience and cultural exchanges with other Mediterranean civilizations. It all begins with the creation of "macere," the retaining walls that make up the cultivable area of the terrace. These walls are made with a skillful arrangement of local stones, with a maximum thickness at the base that decreases as one moves upward. Each wall is finished with a touch of lime that compacts the entire structure. The terraces are not only a work of agricultural engineering but also a sophisticated hydraulic system for rainwater drainage. This water is collected in tanks called "peschiere" and used for irrigation.

The Sfusato lemon has become an indispensable element in high-quality cuisine and a cornerstone of local gastronomy. The recognition of the Protected Geographical Indication (I.G.P.) mark has ensured the protection of the production and marketing of this citrus treasure, thus safeguarding a centuries-old tradition. Today, the lemon groves of the Coast are also a fascinating tourist destination where visitors can discover the natural and cultural beauties of this land and savor the authentic flavors of local lemons. The journey is long and challenging, but the passion and love for this tradition persist, keeping the delicate balance of the Amalfi landscape alive. This is the story of strength, tenacity, and dedication that lies behind every Amalfi Sfusato lemon.

Limoncello is so much more than just a beverage; it is an expression of the passion, history, and culture of this captivating coastal region. Its evolution is a testament to its growing popularity and its ability to captivate palates worldwide with its vibrant flavor and its history steeped in legends and traditions.

SCENTS OF THE COAST: THE LEMON AS CULTURAL AND CULINARY ICON

Lemon, known scientifically as Citrus Limon, belongs to the Rutaceae family and is a member of the Citrae group, Citrinae subgroup, in the sapindale order of dicotyledonous plants, belonging to the angiosperm division. Its scientific classification highlights its significance within the plant kingdom and its role in the production of one of Italy's most iconic beverages, Limoncello.

The structure of the Lemon is complex and diverse, and it is important to understand it fully to appreciate the complexity of the flavors and aromas that this remarkable fruit can offer.

Peel and Epicarp: The outer part of the lemon consists of a thick peel, known as the epicarp or exocarp. This outer layer is usually not edible as it has an unappealing taste, except in the case of kumquats. The surface of the peel is covered by a layer of epicuticular waxes, which can vary in quantity depending on the lemon variety, weather conditions, and the growth process. These waxes are arranged in small plates, forming the outermost epidermal layer. This epidermis often hosts a microflora of fungi and bacteria, which can be more abundant in humid climates. Therefore, it's always essential to thoroughly wash lemons before proceeding with juice and essential oil extraction to remove any contaminants from the fruit's surface.

Just below the outermost epidermis is the flavedo, a peripheral part of the peel. This layer is characterized by colors that can range from yellow to green to yellow and is composed of a few layers of cells that progressively increase in size towards the interior. Here, numerous oil vesicles containing specific essential oils are found. These vesicles, with thin and fragile walls, contain essential oils under positive pressure, allowing their recovery through abrasion of the flavedo layer.

At full ripeness, the flavedo contains carotenoids, primarily xanthophylls, which give the lemon its characteristic yellow color. This part of the peel adds depth of flavor and aroma to the final beverage.

Albedo: Below the flavedo, we find the albedo or mesocarp. This layer is white in color and has a spongy texture. It consists of layers of tubular-shaped cells that, near the endocarp, form a less compact cellular tissue with irregularly shaped intercellular spaces. The albedo contains most of the vascular network that supplies the fruit with water and nutrients. The thickness of the albedo can vary depending on the type of citrus and the cultivar. It's important to adjust the extraction appropriately to account for the thickness of the albedo layer, as it contains flavonoids that, if transferred to the juice, could make it bitter.

Endocarp and Pulp: The endocarp is the central part of the lemon and consists of wedge-shaped segments, or locules, arranged radially. Each locule is covered by a membrane that encloses large multicellular vesicles containing lemon juice. These vesicles are unique juice reservoirs and are not connected through direct vascularization. Their nutrition occurs through the stem tissues. The stem itself contains radially arranged vascular bundles that connect to the vascular elements of the peel. The innermost part of the fruit, known as the core, is composed of spongy tissue similar to that of the albedo.

Endocarpo

This detailed study of the Lemon's structure reveals how complex and precious this fruit is. It is precisely this complexity that gives the Lemon its extraordinary versatility in the kitchen and the ability to be the star of iconic beverages like Limoncello.

THE IMPORTANCE OF LEMONS IN ITALY

Lemons are not just a common fruit in Italy; they play a significant role in the country's culture, cuisine, and agriculture. The presence of lemons is deeply rooted in Italy's identity, contributing to the creation of unique dishes, beverages, and products that carry the flavor of the Mediterranean. Lemons have a long and rich history in Italy. The cultivation of lemons has been documented since ancient Roman times when they were appreciated for their aromatic and therapeutic properties. Over the centuries, lemons have become an integral part of Italian culinary culture. They are found in many traditional recipes, from pasta with seafood to the famous dessert, "Lemon of Sorrento" or "sfusato amalfitano." Lemon cultivation is a pillar of rural economies in many Italian regions, especially on the Amalfi Coast, in Sorrento, and on the island of Capri. Lemon cultivation in these areas has been passed down from generation to generation, and the Mediterranean climate, with its sunny days and cool nights, provides ideal conditions for producing high-quality lemons. The art of lemon processing has given rise to a wide range of Italian artisanal products, including Limoncello. This liqueur, prepared with care and dedication using fresh, local lemons, has become a symbol of Italian hospitality. In addition to

Limoncello, lemons are used to create jams, sauces, creams, and desserts that are beloved worldwide.

LEMONS AND TOURISM

Lemons and Limoncello have become an essential tourist attraction in Italy, adding a touch of magic to the already breathtaking landscape and rich cultural history of the country.

Tourist Destination: The presence of picturesque lemon groves with their perfectly aligned terraces offers visitors a unique experience. The Amalfi Coast, in particular, is famous for its lemons, which adorn the landscape and are often used to decorate the streets during local celebrations. These picturesque views attract tourists from around the world eager to immerse themselves in the beauty of lemon groves and taste products made from fresh lemons.

Lemon Products: In addition to the visual beauty of lemon groves, tourists can savor a wide range of lemon-based products. Farm tours allow visitors to learn the secrets of Limoncello production and taste this delicious liqueur in an authentic setting. Moreover, lemons are often at the center of local events and festivals where tourists can enjoy local lemon-based specialties.

Souvenirs and Gifts: Limoncello and other lemon-based products have become popular gift items for tourists visiting Italy. Bottles of Limoncello decorated with picturesque labels and the vibrant flavor of Italian lemons are sought after as souvenirs to take home. Additionally, lemon creams and sauces are often appreciated as high-quality gastronomic gifts.

In summary, lemons and Limoncello have an extraordinary presence in Italy, both in culture and agriculture, and have become a fundamental part of the country's tourist appeal. Their visual beauty, culinary richness, and connection to Italian tradition make them an essential element for anyone visiting Italy.

SECRET RECIPE FOR THE PERFECT LIMONCELLO

In this chapter, we will reveal how to arrive at the perfect recipe for making Limoncello to share with friends or savor on your own. Get ready to discover the secrets of this iconic Italian beverage and immerse yourself in its millennia-old tradition. Making homemade Limoncello is more than just mixing ingredients; it's a ritual, a testament to Italian art and passion for food and conviviality. We will share with you every detail, from selecting the right lemons to the correct amount of sugar, and guide you step by step through the process of creating this citrus delight. But remember, the true magic of homemade Limoncello lies not only in its ingredients but also in the patient waiting as the liqueur acquires its distinctive flavor. So, get ready to embark on a sensory journey, experience the art of creating the perfect Limoncello, and share the joy of this experience with your loved ones. Without further ado, let's explore the secret recipe for homemade Limoncello.

SELECTING LEMONS

The choice of lemons plays a crucial role in creating Limoncello. It is essential to opt for high-quality organic lemons, preferably of the "femminello" variety, which offer the best flavor profile. These lemons mature in two main blooms: the first between November and January and the second between March and April. It is advisable to harvest the lemons during the early stage of ripening for the best results.

During the selection, you can take a personalized approach. You can choose less ripe lemons with green peel for a fresher and more citrusy flavor or fully ripe ones with completely yellow peel for a sweeter and fuller taste. Each lemon variety will contribute unique flavor nuances to the final Limoncello.

To preserve the freshness and integrity of the lemons, it's essential to work with them within 24 hours of harvesting. During transport, avoid rough handling to prevent the loss of essential oils. Careful selection of lemons is the first step in creating exceptional Limoncello, rich in aroma and taste.

WASHING LEMONS

To prepare excellent Limoncello, it's crucial to start with a thorough cleaning of the lemons. Follow these simple steps to ensure maximum hygiene:

Rinse under water: Begin by thoroughly washing the lemons under a running stream of water. This will help remove any surface dirt residues.

Pat dry: After rinsing, carefully pat dry each lemon with absorbent paper. Ensure you do this gently without rubbing the peel, as it could cause the rupture of surface vesicles and loss of essential oils.

This washing and drying process will ensure the lemons are ready to be used safely and hygienically in Limoncello preparation, preserving the precious aroma of their essential oils.

PEELING LEMONS

Use a potato peeler to remove only the yellow part of the lemon peel, being careful to avoid the underlying white part known as the "albedo." This area can impart an undesirable bitter taste to Limoncello. The yellow part of the peel is particularly valuable as it's rich in essential oils that will give your Limoncello its distinctive aroma and flavor.

The quantity of lemon peels is an important factor that affects the flavor profile of your Limoncello. While many online recipes simply mention the number of lemons to use, this is not an accurate method of quantifying the ingredients in our recipe. It is essential to weigh the lemon peels to achieve a repeatable recipe that produces consistent results.

The recommended range is 150 to 300 grams of lemon peels per liter of alcohol. With 150 grams, you will get a more delicate and light flavor, while with 300 grams, you will have a more intense and robust flavor. The choice depends on your personal preferences and the intended use of the Limoncello. For example, you might opt for 300 grams if you plan to use it in cocktails, while you might prefer a lower quantity for straight sipping.

Start with 200 grams of lemon peels if you want a good balance between delicacy and flavor intensity. You can then experiment with quantities to find your ideal and personalized combination.

PREPARING THE ALCOHOL

Begin by carefully placing the lemon peels in a large glass jar and pour over them a liter of high-proof pure alcohol (at least 95% alcohol). Make sure to fill the jar as much as possible to minimize contact of the peels with the air. This step is essential for proper extraction of essential oils and flavors from the lemons.

An important note regarding the choice of the jar: it's advisable to use dark glass jars as the oils and aromatic components of the lemons are sensitive to light. If you don't have dark jars, you can protect the jar by wrapping it in kitchen foil or storing it in a dark place, such as a closed cupboard.

Seal the jar tightly and place it in a dark and cool location. During the maceration period, occasionally stir the contents to ensure even distribution of flavors. The maceration period is a key aspect in Limoncello preparation, as it will determine the final flavor intensity.

Extraction times can vary, but it's important to know that the process occurs quite rapidly. It's scientifically proven that lemon peels are fully extracted in alcohol in just three days. Moreover, in as little as one day, about 70% of the aromatic components are extracted.

So, if you want a fresh and delicate Limoncello, one day of maceration is sufficient. However, if you're looking for a full and intense flavor, you can let the lemon peels macerate for a maximum of three days. Many recipes suggest longer maceration periods, such as several weeks, but it's important to note that beyond a certain point, it may not significantly improve the flavor. Therefore, the choice of maceration period depends on your personal taste.

SUGAR SYRUP PREPARATION AND MIXING

Sugar is a crucial element in liquor-making as it serves two fundamental purposes: sweetening and adding body to the liquor. The amount of sugar you use will significantly impact the flavor and consistency of the Limoncello. Generally, it's recommended to use pure sucrose sugar, such as white cane sugar or beet sugar. While you can also use raw or unrefined sugar, it's important to note that these types of sugar can alter the flavor of the finished product and affect its color.

Typically, the recommended sugar range is from 100 to 300 grams of sugar per liter of Limoncello. Keep in mind that 100 grams per liter represent the minimum value that defines a liquor; therefore, Limoncello with less than 100 grams of sugar per liter would be very dry. On the other hand, approaching 300 grams per liter will result in a denser, creamier, and sweeter product. An intermediate and often recommended value is around 200 grams of sugar per liter of Limoncello.

The amount of sugar to use will depend on your personal preferences for flavor and the desired consistency of your Limoncello. An important aspect to consider is the alcoholic and sugary content, which can vary significantly depending on the amount of sugar syrup used in the mixture.

To calculate the alcohol content of Limoncello, you can use the following formula:

$$Alcohol\ Content\ (°) = \frac{Alcool\ (ml) * Content(°)}{Quantity\ of\ Limoncello\ (ml)}$$

Usually, the recommended alcohol content is around 20% Vol, which means that 20% of the final liquid will be alcohol.

Example

If you want to create an aromatic Limoncello with an alcohol content of 24% Vol and a sugar content of 200 grams per liter, you can use the following recipe:

- 1 liter of high-proof pure alcohol (at least 95% alcohol)
- 1 kg of organic lemons (200 grams of peels), preferably Sorrento lemons or similar varieties, with thick, pesticide-free, or wax-free peel
- 0.8 kg of white beet sugar
- 2.5 liters of low mineral content water
- To calculate the required amount of sugar and water, keep the following in mind:

Water has a specific weight of 1 gr/ml, which means that 1 kg of water corresponds to 1 liter of water.

The specific weight of alcohol is based on its proof. For example, if you purchase 1 liter of 95% alcohol, you have 950 ml of alcohol and 50 ml of water.

Sugar has a specific weight of 1.59 (or approximately 1.6), which means that if you dissolve 1 kg of sugar in 1 liter of water, the volume of the syrup obtained will be 1,600 ml. That is, the sum of the water volume (1000 ml) and the volume of the dissolved sugar obtained by dividing the weight of sugar (1000 gr) by its specific weight (1.59).

Using this data, you can calculate the alcohol percentage of the Limoncello obtained.

- 1 liter of 95% alcohol will have a volume of 950 ml
- 2.5 liters of water will have a volume of 2,500 ml + 50 ml (contained in the liter of alcohol), so 2,550 ml
- 800 grams of sugar generate a volume of 800/1.6, which is 500 ml

Therefore, the final volume of the Limoncello obtained will be the sum of 950 + 2,550 + 500, which is 4,000 ml (4 liters) at an alcohol content of approximately 24% Vol (a value obtained by dividing the total alcohol by the total volume of the liqueur, 95 x 1000 / 4,000 = 23.7%) and a sugar content of 200 grams per liter (800 grams/4 liters).

To prepare the sugar syrup, start by heating 2.5 liters of water in a basin or pot, being careful not to let it boil. Dissolve 800 grams of sugar in the heated water and stir until you get a homogeneous solution. Let it cool completely.

After the lemon peels have macerated in alcohol for the required time, proceed with filtering the liqueur to remove the peels. If you notice any impurities or suspended particles, you can use coffee or liquor filters along with a funnel for more accurate filtering. It's not advisable to add lemon juice to Limoncello as essential oil can deteriorate over time, especially due to light and acidic environments.

Below, you'll find references to Limoncello from the Amalfi and Sorrento Coasts, and as you can see, the differences between the two liqueurs are minimal, as it mainly changes the type of lemon, the minimum alcohol content, and, of course, the production area. But they both follow basic rules.

Limoncello from the Amalfi Coast must have the following characteristics:

- Produced by cold maceration in IGP Amalfi Coast lemon alcohol
- Must have a minimum alcohol content of 25% Vol
- Sugar content per liter should range from 200 to 350 grams
- For every liter of the finished product, a minimum of 250 grams of lemon peels must be used
- Aromas, emulsifiers, colorants, and stabilizers cannot be added
- It must be produced entirely in the areas of the Amalfi Coast

Limoncello from Sorrento must have these characteristics:

- Produced by cold maceration in IGP Sorrento lemon alcohol
- Must have a minimum alcohol content of 30% Vol
- Sugar content per liter should range from 200 to 350 grams
- For every liter of the finished product, a minimum of 250 grams of lemon peels must be used
- Aromas, emulsifiers, colorants, and stabilizers cannot be added
- It must be produced entirely in the areas of the Sorrento Coast

BOTTLE AND STORAGE

Before bottling your precious Limoncello, it's essential to ensure the impeccable cleanliness of the bottles. An effective method for sterilizing them is to immerse them in a pot of boiling water. This operation should last for at least 20 minutes, after which you can simply drain them while keeping them upside down. To preserve the integrity of your Limoncello, you can seal the bottles with aluminum foil after sterilization, thus preventing contact with air. Now, carefully transfer your Limoncello into the prepared glass bottles and make sure to seal them tightly. After this crucial step, allow your Limoncello to rest, preferably for a period of at least two or three weeks in a cool, dark place before serving.

Traditionally, Limoncello is a digestive liqueur to be enjoyed cold, in small quantities, and in liqueur glasses. To fully appreciate its freshness, we recommend storing it in the freezer, but don't worry, it won't freeze. Once it's ready, you'll have the pleasure of savoring your Limoncello cold, just as tradition dictates.

During the preparation process, make sure to shake the jar a couple of times a day to keep the mixture homogeneous. It's possible that some lemon essential oils may separate from the solution, forming a thin layer on the liquor's surface. This can happen if you've used too many lemon peels in relation to the desired alcohol content. Don't worry, you can gently remove this layer with absorbent paper or a cotton swab, being careful not to waste any of the precious liquid.

CREATING A LIMONCELLO INDEX CALCULATOR IN EXCEL

Creating a Limoncello Index Calculator in Excel is an interesting process that can help monitor the homemade production of this beverage. To begin, it's important to identify the key indicators you want to track, such as the quantity of lemons used, the alcohol level, sugar level, and other critical factors. Once these indicators are identified, I'll explain how to create an Excel worksheet to automate these calculations. This way, you can have complete control over the quality and consistency of your Limoncello, ensuring a delightful and consistent end result.

Monitoring the water, alcohol, and sugar mixture can involve a series of indicators and parameters depending on the goals and properties you want to analyze. Here are some common indicators:

Density: The density of the solution can be monitored to check how much matter is present in the mixture. A change in density can indicate a variation in sugar concentration.

Sweetness Level: If you are looking to measure the sweetness of the solution, you can use methods like a refractometer or a calculation formula based on sugar concentration.

Sugar Concentration: If sweetness is the primary interest, directly monitoring sugar concentration (measured in grams of sugar per unit volume) is essential.

Alcohol Content: If it's important to track the amount of alcohol in the mixture, measure alcohol concentration (in percentage by volume or weight).

Organoleptic Properties: You can perform sensory tests to evaluate aspects such as taste, smell, and visual appearance of the mixture. To measure the organoleptic properties of a mixture, you need to use human senses and sensory tests. Here are some key indicators:

- Taste: Tasters taste the mixture and evaluate the taste in terms of sweetness, bitterness, acidity, saltiness, or any other desired characteristic.
- Smell: Olfactory analysis involves smelling the mixture and describing its aromatic characteristics.
- Color: Color evaluation involves describing the color of the mixture using color standards or grading scales.
- Visual Appearance: Observe the visual appearance of the mixture, including features like clarity, the presence of particles or sediments, and uniformity.
- Texture: Texture refers to the tactile perception of the mixture, such as viscosity or creaminess.
- Stability: Monitor the stability of the mixture over time. Check if significant changes in solution properties occur, such as phase separation or precipitation. The stability of a mixture can be monitored through a series of observations and tests over time. Stability refers to the ability of a mixture to maintain its desired physical, chemical, and organoleptic properties over time without undergoing significant changes.

Now, let's proceed with calculating the parameters in Excel:

Scenario	ml Alcohol	° Alcohol Content	gr/100ml Lemons	ml Water	gr Sugar	gr Lemon Peel	% Sweetness	l Limoncello
1	1000	95	100	1000	1000	200	36	2,6
2	1000	95	100	1400	700	200	24	2,8
3	1000	95	100	1500	900	200	28	3,1
4	1000	95	100	1250	750	200	27	2,7
5	1000	95	100	1300	700	200	25	2,7
6	1000	95	100	1700	700	200	22	3,1
7	1000	95	100	2500	800	200	20	4,0
8	1000	95	100	1800	650	200	20	3,2
9	1000	95	100	1800	600	200	19	3,2
10	1000	95	100	2500	800	200	20	4,0

xsl Table Example

Limoncello (l)

Limoncello parameter indicates the liters of obtained product; this value can be calculated as follows:

$$\text{Limoncello (l)} = \frac{\text{Alcohol(ml)} + \text{Water(ml)} + \text{Sugar dissolved(ml)}}{1000}$$

Where

$$\text{Sugar dissolved (ml)} = \frac{\text{Quantity of Sugar (gr)}}{1,59}$$

Density (gr/ml)

The density of a solution composed of alcohol, water, and sugar depends on the sugar concentration in the solution. The formula to calculate the density parameter of this solution is as follows:

$$\text{Density (gr/ml)} = \frac{\text{Mass of the Solution (gr)}}{\text{Total Solution Volume (ml)}}$$

Where the mass of the solution can be calculated by adding the mass of water, alcohol, and sugar:

Mass of the Solution (gr) = Mass of Water (gr) + Mass of Alcohol (gr) + Mass of Sugar (gr)

Example

The density of alcohol is about 0.789 gr/ml, water is about 1 gr/ml, and sugar's density is considered as its weight. However, the density of the mixture will depend on the proportion of each component. Let's say you're mixing 1.000 ml of alcohol with 1.000 ml of water and adding 1.000 gr of sugar. The total mass of the mixture will then be 2,789 kg. To calculate the density, you need to divide this mass by the total volume of the mixture, which is 2 liters (2.000 ml).

$$\text{Density} = \frac{(1000 * 0{,}789) + (1000 * 1) + (1000)}{(1000 + 1000)} = \frac{2{,}789 \text{ kg}}{2000 \text{ ml}} = 1{,}3945 \; kg/L$$

So, the density of this mixture is approximately 1.3945 kg/liter, which is higher than the density of pure water but lower than that of sugar alone. To understand how dense a liquid is and how to compare it to other liquids, you can use a relative density scale or a specific density scale. Relative density is the ratio between the density of a given liquid and the density of water. The density of water at room temperature is about 1 gr/ml or 1 kg/liter, so you can use it as a reference point. Here's how to calculate the relative density of a liquid:

$$\text{Relative Density} = \frac{\text{Liquid Density}}{\text{Water Density}}$$

In your case, the density of the alcohol, water, and sugar mixture is about 1.3945 kg/liter, as calculated earlier. Now, we can calculate the relative density concerning water:

$$\text{Relative Density} = 1{,}3945 \; / \; 1 = 1{,}3945$$

So, the relative density of this mixture concerning water is approximately 1.3945. This means that the mixture is about 1.3945 times denser than water. To compare the relative density of this mixture with other liquids, you can perform the same calculation for those other liquids and then compare the results. For example, if you want to compare the density of this mixture with that of vegetable oil, which has a density of around 0.92 kg/liter, you can calculate the relative density concerning water and then compare the two values:

$$\text{Relative Density of Vegetable Oil} = 0{,}92 \text{ kg/l} / 1 \text{ kg/l} = 0{,}92$$

So, vegetable oil has a relative density of 0.92 compared to water, while the mixture has a relative density of 1.3945. This means that the mixture is denser than vegetable oil but less dense than water. You can use this method to compare the density of this mixture with other liquids in a similar manner. To give you an idea of how this density fits on a common density scale, here's an example of a density scale for various materials:

- Air at room temperature: Approximately 0.0012 gr/ml
- Water at room temperature: Approximately 1 gr/ml
- Vegetable oil: Approximately 0.92 gr/ml
- Ethyl alcohol (ethanol): Approximately 0.789 gr/ml
- Sugar (sucrose): Approximately 1.59 gr/ml

In general, the higher the density of a solution, the denser and heavier it is compared to water, which has a reference density of 1 gr/ml.

Sugar Concentration (gr/l)

To calculate the sugar concentration in a solution, you need to know the amount of sugar in grams and the volume of the solution in liters or milliliters in which it is dissolved. With this information, you can use the following formula:

$$\text{Sugar Concentration (gr/l)} = \frac{\text{Mass of Sugar (gr)}}{\text{Total Solution Volume (ml)}}$$

For example, let's say you're mixing 1.000 ml of alcohol with 1.000 ml of water and adding 1.000 grams of sugar. You can calculate the sugar concentration as follows:

$$\text{Sugar Concentration} = \frac{1000}{1000 + 1000} = 500 gr/l$$

Sweetness Level (%)

You can estimate the sweetness level of your solution using an approximate formula based on the sugar concentration and the solution's density. This formula assumes that sucrose is the only solute contributing to sweetness. Here's the formula to calculate the sweetness level:

$$\text{Sweetness Level (\%)} = \frac{\text{Mass of Sugar (gr)}}{\text{Total Mass of the Solution (gr)}} \times 100$$

Calculate the total mass of the solution by adding the mass of water, alcohol, and sugar together:

Total Mass of the Solution (gr) = Mass of Water (gr) + Mass of Alcohol (gr) + Mass of Sugar (gr)

Remember:

Mass of Alcohol (gr) = Alcohol Density × Alcohol Volume

So if you have 1 liter of ethyl alcohol, the mass of alcohol in your mixture will be 789 grams (0.789 gr/ml x 1000 ml).

LIMONCELLO IN THE KITCHEN: EXCEPTIONAL DISHES FOR EVERY OCCASION

Over the years, Limoncello has undergone a transformation, evolving from a delightful after-dinner liqueur into a fundamental ingredient in cooking and mixology. When it comes to using Limoncello in dessert preparation, the only true limit is your imagination. You can use it as a fragrant base for creams, mousses, and panna cotta, as a flavorful addition to pie crusts and cookies, or as a filling for a lemon-flavored cake!

An original idea could be to soak ladyfingers in a bit of Limoncello to create an alternative Tiramisù (perfect for those who don't like coffee). And what about ice creams, semifreddos, and sorbets? These iconic Italian treats can take on an even more traditional tone with the fresh aromas of this product. For enthusiasts of international cuisine, you also have the option of incorporating a bit of liqueur into the basic cheesecake recipe to create a citrusy variant!

It's not just desserts that exploit the flavors of Limoncello: risottos and seafood pasta dishes, for example, are perfectly suited to the hints of this product, as well as fish fillets and recipes featuring white meat, where the cooking can be enhanced with a dash of liqueur.

Each recipe in this chapter is accompanied by detailed Preparation and clearly listed ingredients, ensuring that even beginners can confidently experiment. Whether you're preparing cocktails for a special occasion or simply enjoying a quiet evening, you'll find inspiration and enjoyment in these Limoncello creations.

COCKTAILS BASED ON LIMONCELLO

Limoncello Spritz: The Art of Refreshment with a Touch of Lemon

Limoncello Mojito: Mojito with a Lemon Twist

Limoncello Mule: A Moscow Mule with a Lemon Twist

Black Basil Limoncello: A Cocktail of Elegance and Flavor

Gin Fizz Limoncello: A Spark of Lemon in Your Gin Fizz

Limoncello Sour: The Delicious Bitterness of Lemon

Limoncello Tass: A Dip of Lemon in a Refreshing Cocktail

Limoncello and Mint: A Fresh and Aromatic Harmony

Cucumber, Lemon, and Limoncello: A Trilogy of Freshness

Lemon Drop Martini: A Martini with a Touch of Lemon

Limoncello Bellini: The Sparkling Elegance of Lemon

Limoncello Margarita: A Surprising Lemon Margarita

Christmas Star: A Sparkling Cocktail for the Holidays

FIRST COURSES BASED ON LIMONCELLO

Limoncello Risotto: Risotto Transformed into Citrus Delight

Limoncello Gnocchi: A Symphony of Mediterranean Flavors

Limoncello Tagliolini: Elegance and Flavor in Every Bite

Limoncello Spaghetti with Seafood: An Explosion of Seafood and Citrus Flavors

Paccheri with Shrimp and Limoncello: A Hymn to Marine Freshness

Linguine with Tuna and Olives Limoncello: A Taste Journey in the Mediterranean

Spaghetti with Limoncello and Sardines: A Harmony of Sea and Lemon Flavors

Penne with Salmon and Limoncello: A Gustatory Triumph Between Land and Sea

Limoncello Spaghetti with Bottarga, Lemon, and Sarde: A Mediterranean Symphony of Flavors

Penne with Zucchini and Grana Padano Cream Limoncello: Culinary Harmony Between Land, Lemon, and Cheese

Ravioli with Limoncello and Ricotta: Citrus Elegance in Every Bite

Pappardelle with Limoncello and Asparagus: Audacious Harmony of Mediterranean Flavors

Rigatoni with Limoncello, Cherry Tomatoes, and Basil: A Triumph of Summer Flavors

MAIN COURSES BASED ON LIMONCELLO

Tuna with Limoncello: The Taste of the Sea with a Fresh Touch

Fish Braciole with Limoncello: An Explosion of Mediterranean Aromas

Sturgeon Fillets with Limoncello: Elegance and Flavor in Every Bite

Limoncello-Stuffed Calamari: A Sea Delight with a Surprising Twist

Limoncello Prawns: The Pleasure of the Sea in a Limoncello Harmony

Scampi with Limoncello: Marine Delight with a Touch of Freshness

Salmon with Limoncello: A Flavor Journey Between Land and Sea

Limoncello Sole: Delicate Tastes and a Lemon Twist

Limoncello Branzino: Fish Joins the Freshness of the Amalfi Coast

Limoncello Steak: A Flavor Explosion with a Citrusy Touch

Limoncello Chicken Breast: Taste and Sweetness in a Single Dish

Limoncello Cornish Hen: A Dance of Flavors with a Limoncello Twist

Pork with Limoncello: A Symphony of Tastes with a Lemon Twist

LIMONCELLO-BASED DESSERTS

Limoncello Tiramisù: An Explosion of Freshness in an Italian Classic

Limoncello-Scented Panna Cotta: Elegance and Sweetness in Every Spoonful

Limoncello Soufflé: Lightness and Lemon Aromas in a Surprising Dessert

Crostata with a Limoncello Heart: Crunchiness Meets Limoncello Creaminess

Limoncello Semifreddo: A Cold Lemon Kiss for Your Taste Buds

Limoncello Cupcakes: Single-Serving Delight with the Freshness of Lemon

Homemade Limoncello Ice Cream: Authentic and Refreshing Taste

Limoncello Cheesecake: Creaminess in Harmony with the Lemon Flavor

Limoncello Sorbet: The Refreshing Symphony to End Your Meal

LIMONCELLO MIXOLOGY: COCKTAILS AND APERITIFS FROM THE SORRENTO AND AMALFI COAST

Limoncello will surprise you, proving to be very versatile in the preparation of cocktails, drinks, and even desserts. In this section, we will immerse ourselves in the world of mixology, where Limoncello, Italy's golden liqueur, becomes the key to exceptional cocktails. From refreshing aperitifs to sophisticated drinks, you will discover how Limoncello can transform into a magical ingredient in anyone's hands. Limoncello cocktails are not just drinks; they are taste experiences that celebrate the richness of Italian flavor. Each blend is a symphony of aromas, a dance of flavors that evoke the beauty of the Mediterranean coasts and the warmth of Italian hospitality. We will guide you through a series of cocktails inspired by tradition and innovation. From unique variations of the classic Limoncello Spritz to the intriguing Limoncello Mojito, we will explore the art of mixing tastes and creating new tasting experiences.

Get ready to raise your glass and toast to Italian excellence with these extraordinary cocktails.

LIMONCELLO SPRITZ

200 ml of Prosecco

100 ml of Soda

30 ml of Limoncello

Ice as desired

Preparation

Chill the glasses: Before you begin, place the Spritz glasses in the freezer or refrigerator to chill them. Limoncello is best when it's very cold, so this will help keep the drink cool longer.

Prepare the ice: You can use regular ice cubes or, if you prefer, make lemon ice cubes for an extra touch of flavor.

Measure the ingredients: Take a jigger and carefully measure the ingredients:

- Pour 30 ml of Limoncello into a Spritz glass.
- Add 200 ml of Prosecco into the same glass.
- Top with 100 ml of Soda.

You can adjust these proportions according to your personal preferences. If you prefer a sweeter drink, you can increase the amount of Limoncello.

Add ice: Add ice to the glass until it's filled to your liking. The ice will not only chill your Spritz but also help to slightly dilute it for a smoother sip.

Gently stir: Use a spoon or a cocktail stirring stick to gently mix the ingredients in the glass. Make sure the Limoncello, Prosecco, and Soda are well blended.

Garnish (optional): If desired, you can garnish your Limoncello Spritz with a slice of lemon or a lemon twist for an extra touch of freshness.

Serve immediately: Your Limoncello Spritz is ready to be enjoyed! Be sure to serve it very cold.

A great fresh and exotic variation can be the Mint and Lime Limoncello Spritz, in which Ice Blanc de Blancs can further enhance the taste of this spice.

MOJITO AL LIMONCELLO

50 ml of White Rum

30 ml of Limoncello

1 lime

6-8 fresh mint leaves

2 teaspoons of brown sugar

Ice as needed

Soda or sparkling water

Lime slice and mint sprig for garnish (optional)

Preparation

Prepare the lime: Cut the lime into wedges or thin slices. Make sure to remove any seeds.

Muddle the mint and sugar: In a tall glass, place the mint leaves and brown sugar. Use a muddler or a spoon to gently crush the mint leaves to release the essential oils.

Add the lime: Add the lime pieces to the glass with the mint and sugar. Also, lightly squeeze the lime to release the juice.

Add Limoncello and Rum: Pour 30 ml of Limoncello and 50 ml of white rum into the glass with the other ingredients.

Add ice: Add ice cubes to the glass until filled to your liking. The ice will cool and dilute the Mojito.

Mix well: Use a long spoon to mix all the ingredients thoroughly in the glass. Make sure the sugar has completely dissolved.

Top with soda: Fill the glass with soda or sparkling water as desired, depending on how much you want to dilute the Mojito. Stir gently.

Garnish (optional): For an appealing presentation, you can garnish your Limoncello Mojito with a lime slice and a fresh mint sprig.

Serve immediately: Your Limoncello Mojito is ready to be enjoyed! Sip it slowly and enjoy this refreshing lemony beverage.

LIMONCELLO MULE

60 ml of Limoncello

15 ml of lemon juice

One strawberry

4 basil leaves

60 ml of Gosling's Ginger Beer

Preparation

Muddle the strawberry and basil: In a cocktail glass, muddle a ripe strawberry and add 4 basil leaves. Gently muddle to release the flavors.

Add the remaining ingredients: Pour 60 ml of Pallini Limoncello and 15 ml of lemon juice into the glass with the strawberry and basil.

Shake well: Fill the glass with ice and mix all the ingredients well.

Top with Gosling's Ginger Beer: Slowly pour 60 ml of Gosling's Ginger Beer into the glass to complete the cocktail.

Garnish: Add a basil leaf as decoration.

Serve: Your Strawberry Basil Limoncello cocktail is ready to be enjoyed! This cocktail offers a combination of freshness from the lemon, sweetness from the strawberry, and an aromatic touch from the basil, all with a hint of ginger from the ginger beer. Cheers!

BLACK BASIL LIMONCELLO

30 ml of Absolut Vodka

30 ml of Lemon Juice

15 ml of Limoncello

15 ml of Syrup

2 fresh Basil Leaves

Ice Cubes

Tonic Water (to top up)

Preparation

Prepare the shaker: Fill a shaker with ice cubes.

Add the ingredients: Pour the following ingredients into the shaker:

- 30 ml of Absolut Vodka
- 30 ml of Lemon Juice
- 15 ml of Limoncello
- 15 ml of Syrup
- 2 fresh Basil Leaves

Shake: Close the shaker and shake vigorously to mix the ingredients well. Shaking will help chill and mix the cocktail.

Strain into the glass: Using a strainer, pour the contents of the shaker into a highball glass previously filled with ice cubes.

Top up with tonic water: Fill the glass with tonic water until it reaches the desired quantity. You can adjust the amount of tonic water to your personal taste.

Garnish (optional): If desired, you can decorate the cocktail with a fresh basil leaf or a lemon slice.

Serve: Your Black Basil Limoncello is ready to be enjoyed! Enjoy this cool and aromatic cocktail.

GIN FIZZ LIMONCELLO

45 ml of Gin

15 ml of Limoncello

15 ml of Fresh Lemon Juice

10 ml of Sugar Syrup

80 ml of Soda Water

Preparation

Add the ingredients: Pour the following ingredients into a shaker:

- 45 ml of Gin
- 15 ml of Limoncello
- 15 ml of Fresh Lemon Juice
- 10 ml of Sugar Syrup

Shake: Close the shaker and shake vigorously to mix the ingredients well. Shaking will help chill and mix the cocktail.

Strain into the glass: Using a strainer, pour the contents of the shaker into a highball glass previously filled with ice cubes.

Top up with soda water: Fill the glass with soda water to your liking, depending on how much you want to dilute the Fizz. Stir gently.

Garnish: You can garnish with a slice of lemon or some mint leaves, as desired.

LIMONCELLO SOUR

60 ml of Midori

30 ml of Limoncello

60 ml of Sweet & Sour (a mixture of sugar and lemon juice)

1 maraschino cherry

Preparation

Prepare the shaker: Fill a shaker with ice cubes.

Add the ingredients: Pour the following ingredients into the shaker:
- 60 ml of Midori
- 30 ml of Limoncello
- 60 ml of Sweet & Sour (a mixture of sugar and lemon juice)

Shake: Close the shaker and shake vigorously to mix the ingredients well and chill the cocktail.

Strain into a Martini glass: Using a strainer, pour the contents of the shaker into a pre-chilled Martini glass.

Garnish: Garnish the cocktail with a maraschino cherry. You can do this by placing the cherry directly in the glass or by skewering it on a small cocktail stick and placing it on the rim of the glass.

Serve: Your Limoncello Sour is ready to be enjoyed! It's a fresh and uniquely flavored cocktail.

LIMONCELLOTASS

150 ml of Cedrata Tassoni

90 ml of Limoncello

60 ml of Aperol

Half a Lemon Slice

Preparation

Fill the glass with ice: Prepare a tall glass and fill it halfway with ice cubes.

Pour the ingredients: Add the ingredients directly into the iced glass in the quantities indicated:

- 150 ml of Cedrata Tassoni
- 90 ml of Limoncello
- 60 ml of Aperol

Stir gently: Use a spoon to gently stir the ingredients in the glass.

Garnish with a lemon slice: To complete the presentation, add half a lemon slice as decoration.

Serve: Your Lemontass is ready to be served and enjoyed. It's a refreshing and uniquely flavored beverage, perfect for summer days.

LIMONCELLO AND MINT

45 ml of Limoncello

30 ml of Gin

150 ml of Lemon Juice

60 ml of Soda Water

10 Mint Leaves

Preparation

Mint and lemon juice: Start by placing the mint leaves and freshly filtered lemon juice in the glass of a shaker. Gently muddle them to release the mint's flavor.

Add Limoncello and Gin: Pour the Limoncello (45 ml) and Gin (30 ml) into the glass with the mint and lemon juice.

Add ice: Fill the shaker with ice.

Shake: Close the shaker and shake vigorously for about 10 seconds. This will mix the ingredients well and chill them.

Strain into the glass: Strain the contents of the shaker into a highball glass filled halfway with ice cubes.

Add Soda: Fill the glass with 60 ml of Soda Water (carbonated water).

Garnish: To finish, garnish the drink with a lemon slice and some mint leaves.

Serve: Your Limoncello and Mint cocktail is ready to be served. It's a refreshing and lively-flavored drink, perfect for the summer.

CUCUMBER, LEMON, AND LIMONCELLO

1 cucumber

45 ml of Limoncello

Juice of 2 lemons (about 120 ml)

6 teaspoons of sugar (or to taste)

10 Mint Leaves

Preparation

Prepare the cucumber and mint: Start by peeling the cucumber, cutting it into pieces, and blending it together with the mint leaves. This should give you about 300 ml of cucumber and mint puree.

Combine the ingredients: Transfer the cucumber and mint puree to a shaker. Add the Limoncello (45 ml), the juice of the two lemons (about 120 ml), and the sugar (according to your personal taste).

Shake: Close the shaker and shake vigorously to mix the ingredients well and cool the mixture.

Pour into glasses: Pour the cocktail into glasses.

Garnish: To decorate, add some mint leaves and/or lemon slices to the glasses.

Serve cold: Your Cucumber, Lemon, and Limoncello cocktail is ready to be served. It's a cool and refreshing drink with a delightful combination of cucumber, lemon, and Limoncello flavors.

LEMON DROP MARTINI

60 ml Limoncello

30 ml vodka

30 ml fresh lemon juice

Sugar for rimming the glass

Lemon slice for garnish

Preparation

Prepare the glass: Dampen the rim of a martini glass by gently running it under tap water, then dip it in a plate of sugar to create a sugar rim on the glass.

Chill the glass: Place the glass in the freezer or fill it with ice to chill while you prepare the cocktail.

Prepare the cocktail: In an ice-filled shaker, pour 60 ml of Limoncello, 30 ml of vodka, and 30 ml of fresh lemon juice.

Shake: Close the shaker and shake vigorously for about 15-20 seconds to chill and mix the ingredients thoroughly.

Strain: Using a strainer, pour the cocktail into the pre-rimmed martini glass, being careful not to disturb the sugar rim.

Garnish: Decorate the cocktail with a lemon slice placed on the rim of the glass or a twist of lemon zest.

Serve: Your Lemon Drop Martini is ready to be enjoyed!

LIMONCELLO BELLINI

60 ml Limoncello

90 ml Prosecco

30 ml peach puree or fresh peach juice

Preparation

Pour the Limoncello into a champagne flute or wine glass.

Add the peach puree or fresh peach juice.

Gently stir.

Top it off with the Prosecco.

Stir again carefully.

You can garnish with a lemon slice or a peach slice if desired.

Serve and enjoy your Limoncello Bellini!

LIMONCELLO MARGARITA

60 ml Limoncello

30 ml tequila

30 ml triple sec

Fresh lime juice

Salt for rimming the glass

Preparation

Dampen the rim of a margarita glass with a lime wedge and then dip it in salt to coat the rim.

In an ice-filled shaker glass, pour the Limoncello, tequila, and triple sec.

Add fresh lime juice. The amount can vary depending on how tart you prefer your Margarita.

Shake the contents of the shaker vigorously to chill and mix the ingredients.

Strain the cocktail into a prepared margarita glass with the salted rim.

If desired, you can add a few fresh ice cubes.

Garnish with a lime slice or lemon slice, according to your preference.

Serve and enjoy your Limoncello Margarita!

STELLA DI NATALE

90 ml white Vermouth

60 ml Limoncello

150 ml Brut Sparkling Wine

Preparation

Pour the liquids into the mixing glass: Start by pouring 60 ml of Lemon Liqueur and 90 ml of White Vermouth into the mixing glass.

Stir: Gently stir the ingredients in the mixing glass.

Pour into a flute: Take a well-chilled flute and pour the mixture into it.

Add the Sparkling Wine: Complete the cocktail by adding 150 ml of Brut Sparkling Wine to the flute.

Garnish: To decorate, you can add a strip of lemon zest on the surface of the cocktail. Now you've prepared the delightful Stella di Natale cocktail. This sparkling drink is perfect for the holiday season. Merry Christmas!

Remember to always drink responsibly.

FIRST COURSES AROMATIZED: THE DELIGHTS OF LIMONCELLO IN THE KITCHEN

This paragraph is a celebration of Italian cuisine, particularly first courses, elevated to new heights of delight thanks to the magical addition of Limoncello. Let the unique flavor of Italian lemons blend with the richness of the culinary traditions of the Bel Paese as we explore a series of extraordinary dishes. In the world of Italian cuisine, first courses represent the very soul of eating well. They are dishes that carry with them the history, culture, and passion of the Campania coast. And now, thanks to Limoncello, these dishes open up new horizons of taste. In this section, we will guide you through a culinary journey that will lead you to discover how Limoncello can transform a simple pasta or risotto dish into an unforgettable gastronomic experience. Each recipe will be a celebration of local flavors and Limoncello, making every bite a journey through the Neapolitan coast.

It doesn't matter if you are an experienced chef or a beginner in the kitchen; these recipes are designed to be accessible to all. With clear Preparation and easily available ingredients, you can experiment with confidence and prepare first-class dishes that will bring the taste of Italy directly to your table. Get ready to delight your senses and discover how amazing Italian cuisine can be when it joins forces with the power of Limoncello.

LEMONCELLO RISOTTO

320 gr of rice

2 tablespoons of Grana Padano cheese

1 small bunch of basil

60 ml of Limoncello

Zest and juice of 1 untreated lemon

30 gr of butter

Extra-virgin olive oil (EVO), as needed

1 liter of vegetable broth

Salt and pepper, to taste

Preparation:

Wash and chop the basil, not too finely, and set it aside.

In a large pan, melt a knob of butter. As soon as the butter starts to sizzle, add the basil and cook over moderate heat.

Add the rice and toast it lightly for a couple of minutes, then increase the heat and deglaze with Limoncello. Continue cooking until you no longer smell the alcohol rising from the pan.

Start adding hot broth, one ladle at a time, so the rice is always just covered. Keep stirring. Add more broth only when the previous ladle has been completely absorbed. Around halfway through cooking, taste the rice and adjust the salt to your liking.

When cooking is complete, add the grated lemon zest. Remove the pan from the heat and stir the risotto with the butter and grated Grana Padano cheese.

Serve the Limoncello Risotto on plates and garnish as desired with fresh basil leaves.

Now you can enjoy your delicious Limoncello Risotto!

LIMONCELLO GNOCCHI

500 gr of fresh or dried gnocchi

Zest and juice of 2 untreated lemons

150 ml of cooking cream

50 ml of Limoncello

2 tablespoons of butter

Salt and freshly ground black pepper, to taste

Grated Parmesan cheese, for serving

Freshly chopped parsley, for garnish (optional)

Preparation:

Gnocchi preparation: If you're using fresh gnocchi, cook them in plenty of salted water according to the package Preparation or until they start to float. If using dried gnocchi, follow the package Preparation for cooking.

Limoncello sauce preparation: In a large pan, melt the butter over medium heat. Add the grated lemon zest and stir for a minute until fragrant.

Add the lemon juice: Make sure you've washed the lemons and grated the zest before extracting the juice and the Limoncello. Cook for another 2-3 minutes, allowing the liquor to evaporate slightly.

Pour the cream into the pan and mix well. Bring to a boil and reduce the heat to low. Let it simmer for about 5 minutes, or until the sauce thickens slightly. Taste and add salt and freshly ground black pepper to your liking.

Finishing the dish:

Drain the cooked gnocchi and transfer them directly to the pan with the Limoncello sauce. Gently toss to coat the gnocchi with the Limoncello sauce.

Serving: Transfer the Limoncello Gnocchi to individual plates. Sprinkle with fresh grated Parmesan cheese, and if desired, garnish with freshly chopped parsley. Serve immediately while it's still hot.

These Limoncello Gnocchi are a deliciously creamy and aromatic dish that captures the fresh essence of lemons. Enjoy!

LIMONCELLO TAGLIOLINI

80 gr of 100% durum wheat semolina

20 gr of Limoncello

3 lemons

20 gr of whole eggs

A small bunch of basil

Extra-virgin olive oil

A knob of butter

1 clove of garlic

Parmesan cheese

Pepper (optional)

Preparation:

Preparing the Limoncello: In a saucepan, pour in the Limoncello and bring it to a boil to evaporate the alcohol. Add lemon zest during this process to infuse flavor. Allow it to cool and remove the lemon zest.

Pasta Dough: In a bowl, combine the durum wheat semolina, evaporated Limoncello, whole eggs, and grated lemon zest. Knead until you have a homogeneous dough. Wrap the dough in plastic wrap and let it rest in the refrigerator for at least 3 hours.

Rolling Out the Pasta: Pass the dough through a pasta rolling machine, making 8 passes until you reach the desired thickness (ideally 0.2-0.3 mm, so it's not too thin to appreciate the flavor). Cut the pasta into tagliolini with a thickness of about 2 mm.

Preparing Lemon Zest: Place the zest of 2 untreated lemons in cold water and refrigerate for at least 24 hours.

Cooking the Pasta: Start heating water in a pot over medium-high heat for cooking the pasta. In a skillet, add a little extra-virgin olive oil, a knob of butter, two lemon zest strips, and a garlic clove (which you can remove later). Add the hot water from the pot and a lemon leaf to flavor the sauce.

Cooking the Tagliolini: Place the tagliolini directly into the skillet with the sauce. Let them cook without touching for about 2 minutes. Then, start gently stirring, adding freshly grated Parmesan cheese and a bit of lemon zest to create a flavorful cream.

Plating: Drain the tagliolini al dente directly onto a serving plate. Add fresh basil leaves as a final touch. If desired, you can also add a sprinkle of freshly ground black pepper for a bit of spiciness.

Now you can enjoy your delicious Limoncello Tagliolini, a fresh and flavorful dish with the unique scent of lemon!

SPAGHETTI WITH LIMONCELLO AND SEAFOOD

320 grams of spaghetti

300 grams of mixed seafood (such as shrimp, mussels, clams, calamari, as desired)

2 cloves of garlic, finely chopped

1 fresh red chili (optional), finely chopped

50 ml of Limoncello

Juice and zest of 2 lemons

3 tablespoons of extra-virgin olive oil

Salt and freshly ground black pepper, to taste

Freshly chopped parsley, for garnish

Preparation:

Cleaning the Seafood: Begin by thoroughly rinsing the seafood under cold running water to remove any sand or debris. Drain them well.

Making the Soffritto: In a large pan, heat the extra-virgin olive oil over medium heat. Add the chopped garlic and red chili (if using) and a few sprigs of parsley. Sauté lightly until the garlic turns golden and the chili releases its aroma, which should take about 1-2 minutes. Add the seafood to the pan and sauté for about 2-3 minutes or until the seafood begins to tenderize and open (in the case of mussels and clams). Remove those that open completely and set them aside.

Limoncello Deglaze: Deglaze the pan with Limoncello and let the alcohol evaporate while gently stirring to combine the flavors. This should take about 2 minutes. Add the lemon juice and the grated lemon zest to the pan. Stir well to combine all the ingredients.

Cooking the Pasta: In a large pot, bring plenty of salted water to a boil. Once the water is boiling, cook the spaghetti following the package Preparation until they are al dente. They are typically ready in 8-10 minutes. Add the cooked spaghetti to the pan with the seafood and Limoncello sauce. Gently toss to ensure the spaghetti is well-seasoned and coated with the sauce.

Adding the Seafood: Add the previously set-aside open seafood on top of the spaghetti and adjust salt and freshly ground black pepper to taste.

Serving: Serve the Spaghetti with Limoncello and Seafood hot, garnishing with finely chopped fresh parsley for a touch of color and freshness.

Now you can savor this delicious seafood pasta with the unique touch of Limoncello!

PACCHERI WITH SHRIMP AND LIMONCELLO

350 gr of paccheri or another type of rough and bronze-drawn pasta

12 prawns

2 cloves of garlic

1 small spring onion or 2 shallots

2 squeezed oranges and 1 for garnish

1 small glass of Limoncello

Fresh mint leaves

Extra-virgin olive oil

Pepper and Salt, to taste

Preparation:

Cleaning the Prawns: Start by thoroughly rinsing the prawns under cold running water to remove any residues. Gently shell 6 of the 12 prawns, keeping aside the whole heads of the other 6.

Squeezing Oranges: If you prefer, squeeze two oranges and set the juice aside for later use.

Making the Soffritto: In a large pan, heat some extra-virgin olive oil over low heat. Add whole garlic cloves and chopped spring onion (or shallots) to the heated oil.

Adding the Prawns: Right after adding the garlic and spring onion, add both the whole prawns and the shelled prawns with their heads to the pan. Sauté with the prawn shells for about 2 minutes or until you can smell the intense prawn aroma. While sautéing the shells, gently crush the heads with a spoon to release all their aroma. Add salt to taste to flavor.

Alcohol Deglazing: Pour the glass of Limoncello into the pan with the prawns. Increase the flame to let the Limoncello's alcohol evaporate. This process should take about 1 minute. Make sure to gently mix while the alcohol evaporates.

Adding Orange Juice: After the alcohol evaporates, lower the flame and incorporate the squeezed orange juice. If you prefer not to use orange juice, you can also add a ladle of pasta cooking water instead.

Add whole pepper grains for a touch of spiciness.

Covering and Cooking: Cover the pan with a lid and let it simmer over low heat for about 10 minutes. This will allow the prawns to cook in a Limoncello and orange aromatic sauce. After 10 minutes, you can choose between two alternative methods: either blend the stock (also known as bisque, it's the rich broth prepared using prawn heads and shells to season first courses and make them creamier), then strain it through a fine mesh sieve for a thicker bisque, or strain the stock directly, without blending, for a thinner bisque. Your prawn bisque will be ready to cream the paccheri dish.

Pasta: In the meantime, cook the pasta in boiling salted water until it reaches your desired level of doneness. Remember to drain it al dente so it can cook for a few more minutes in the pan to better absorb the sauce.

Final Assembly: When the pasta is ready, add it to the pan with the prawns and sauce. Gently mix to combine the ingredients. Add fresh mint leaves for a touch of freshness.

Serving: Serve the Paccheri with Shrimp and Limoncello hot. Use the whole prawns set aside earlier to garnish the dish. You can also add thin orange slices as a final decoration if you like.

This dish is a seafood delight with the unique touch of Limoncello and orange. Enjoy!

LINGUINE LIMONCELLO WITH TUNA AND OLIVES

200 grams of linguine

80 grams of canned tuna in oil

1 clove of garlic

2 fillets of anchovies in oil

20 pitted black olives

2 tablespoons of Limoncello

Zest of one lemon

Preparation:

Preparing the Ingredients: Start by cutting the garlic clove in half and sautéing it in a little olive oil in a large pan. Once the garlic is golden, remove it from the pan.

Adding Anchovies and Tuna: Add the anchovy fillets in oil to the pan with the flavored oil. Let the anchovy fillets dissolve in the pan, stirring gently.

Tuna and Olives: Add the canned tuna to the pan with the anchovies. Cut the black olives in half and add them to the pan as well. Cook the ingredients for about 1 minute to allow them to meld.

Boiling Linguine with Lemon Zest: Meanwhile, in a separate pot, bring slightly salted water to a boil. Add lemon zest to the boiling water to flavor the pasta. This will give a delightful aroma to the pasta.

Cooking the Pasta: Add the linguine to the pot with the boiling water and lemon zest. Cook the linguine following the package Preparation but leave 3-5 minutes of cooking to complete the process in the pan with the sauce. Before draining the pasta, make sure to reserve a bit of cooking water and set it aside.

Creaming the Pasta: Transfer the linguine directly to the pan with the tuna, anchovies, and olives. Add the Limoncello to the sauce and mix well. As the pasta begins to dry, gradually add the reserved cooking water to keep everything moist. Continue to cook the pasta in the pan, stirring gently.

Grated Lemon Zest: At the end of cooking, garnish the pasta with the grated zest of one lemon. Make sure to use only a small amount of zest as it is highly aromatic.

Serving: Serve the Linguine with Limoncello, Tuna, and Olives hot, perhaps with a sprig of fresh mint as a garnish.

This dish is a burst of Mediterranean flavors with the unique touch of Limoncello and grated lemon zest.

SPAGHETTI WITH LIMONCELLO AND SARDINES

350 grams of spaghetti

8 sardines

200 grams of stale bread

1 small cup of Limoncello

Parsley and Salt, to taste

Fennel fronds, to taste

Extra-virgin olive oil, to taste

1 clove of garlic

Red pepper flakes (optional, to taste)

Preparation:

Making Flavored Breadcrumbs: Blend the stale bread with garlic, parsley, salt, fennel fronds, and red pepper flakes (if desired). Mix in Limoncello and a drizzle of olive oil to create flavored breadcrumbs.

Preparing the Sardines: Clean the sardines, removing their insides and bones. Sauté the sardines in a pan with a bit of hot oil until they are well browned. Remove the sardines from the pan and set them aside.

Cooking the Pasta: Boil the spaghetti in salted water and drain them al dente. In a pan, heat some oil using that from the sardines. Add the drained spaghetti and toss them in the sardine oil. Add the flavored breadcrumbs and mix well to combine all the ingredients.

Plating: Plate the spaghetti, garnishing with two sautéed sardines on top. Add a sprinkle of fresh parsley for decoration.

Now you can enjoy Spaghetti with Limoncello and Sardines, a dish with a unique and Mediterranean flavor!

PENNETTE WITH SALMON AND LIMONCELLO

160 grams of penne

100 grams of natural salmon fillet

70 ml of vegetable broth

1 shallot

A pinch of red pepper flakes

1 sprig of parsley

2 sprigs of chives

Salt, to taste

Extra-virgin olive oil, to taste

Preparation:

Preparing the Salmon: Begin by finely chopping the parsley and chives. Thinly slice the shallot. In a large pan, heat three tablespoons of extra-virgin olive oil over medium heat. Add the sliced shallot and sauté until it becomes translucent, reducing the heat if necessary. Gradually add the vegetable broth to the pan with the shallot. Allow it to cook until almost all the broth is consumed. Add a pinch of red pepper flakes and deglaze with a generous splash of Limoncello. Let it cook for another minute or two until the liquid has slightly reduced and thickened. Coarsely chop the salmon fillet. Add the salmon to the pan with the Limoncello, shallot, and broth. Gently mix to warm the salmon, being careful not to overcook it. Adjust the salt, if needed. Add the chopped parsley and chives, mixing everything well.

Cooking the Pasta: Meanwhile, cook the penne in salted boiling water following the package Preparation until al dente. Drain them but keep a small amount of the pasta cooking water aside. Add the cooked penne to the pan with the salmon and sauce. If the sauce is too thick, you can add some of the reserved pasta cooking water. Mix everything well so that the penne are well seasoned. Off the heat, you can grate some lemon zest over the dish to enhance the lemon aroma if desired.

Now, your Penne with Salmon and Limoncello are ready to be served. Enjoy!

SPAGHETTI WITH BOTTARGA, LEMON, AND LIMONCELLO

320 grams of spaghetti

50 grams of grated bottarga

Grated zest of 1 untreated lemon

50 ml of Limoncello

3 tablespoons of extra-virgin olive oil (EVO)

Freshly ground black pepper, to taste

Salt, to taste

Chopped fresh parsley (for garnish, optional)

Preparation:

Bring a pot of salted water to a boil and cook the spaghetti according to the package Preparation until al dente.

Meanwhile, in a large pan, heat the extra-virgin olive oil over medium heat. Add the grated lemon zest and briefly sauté it to release its aromas, making sure not to let it burn.

Add the grated bottarga to the pan with the olive oil and lemon. Mix well to allow it to melt slightly.

Drain the spaghetti al dente, making sure to reserve a small amount of cooking water. Add the spaghetti directly to the pan with the oil, bottarga, and lemon. Also, add the Limoncello.

Mix everything well over medium heat, adding a couple of tablespoons of cooking water to create a velvety cream. Continue to stir until the spaghetti are well coated with the sauce and the Limoncello has been absorbed. Adjust for salt, if necessary, and season with freshly ground black pepper.

Transfer the Spaghetti with Bottarga, Lemon, and Limoncello to serving plates. Garnish with chopped fresh parsley, if desired. Serve immediately and enjoy this gourmet dish with a special touch of Limoncello.

PENNE WITH LIMONCELLO AND ZUCCHINI WITH CHEESE CREAM

320gr of penne

2 medium zucchinis, diced

60ml of Limoncello

200ml of fresh cream

50g of grated Grana Padano cheese

30g of butter

Grated lemon zest (from 1 lemon)

Salt and pepper, to taste

Preparation:

In a large pan, melt a knob of butter and cook the diced zucchinis until they become golden.

Deglaze with a touch of Limoncello, allowing the alcohol to evaporate. Add the fresh cream and the grated lemon zest to the pan. Let it cook over medium-low heat until the sauce slightly thickens. Make sure to mix well.

Cook the penne al dente following the package Preparation. Drain and add the cooked penne to the pan with the zucchini and Limoncello cream. Mix well to blend the flavors. Complete the dish with the grated Grana Padano cheese and a generous grind of black pepper.

Serve the Penne with Limoncello and Zucchini hot and garnish, if desired, with a bit of freshly grated lemon zest for a touch of freshness.

RAVIOLI WITH LIMONCELLO AND RICOTTA

350-400gr of ricotta and spinach ravioli (store-bought or homemade)

1/4 cup (about 60 ml) of Limoncello

4-5 tablespoons of butter

Grated zest of 1 lemon

1/2 cup of grated Pecorino Romano cheese

2 tablespoons of chopped fresh parsley

Salt and pepper, to taste

Preparation:

Cook the ravioli in abundant salted water following the package Preparation or until they are al dente. Usually, it will take about 2-3 minutes if they are fresh or a bit longer if they are frozen or store-bought.

Meanwhile, in a large pan, melt the butter over medium-low heat. Make sure not to let the butter burn. Add the grated lemon zest to the pan and the Limoncello. Sauté lightly for a minute until the alcohol evaporates, and the butter has absorbed the lemon flavor.

When the ravioli are ready, drain them and transfer them to the pan with the Limoncello butter. Gently mix to coat the ravioli with the fragrant sauce. Add the grated Pecorino Romano cheese and a pinch of salt and pepper to taste. Continue to mix until the ravioli are well seasoned and enveloped in the creamy sauce.

Sprinkle chopped fresh parsley over the ravioli as a final touch. Serve your delicious Ravioli with Limoncello and Ricotta hot and savor this aromatic and flavorful delicacy!

PAPPARDELLE WITH LIMONCELLO AND ASPARAGUS

300g of fresh or dried pappardelle

200g of fresh asparagus, cut into pieces

60 ml of Limoncello

60g of grated Parmesan cheese

2 tablespoons of butter

1 teaspoon of freshly grated ginger

Grated zest of 1 lemon

Salt and freshly ground black pepper, to taste

Fresh ginger and lemon zest for garnish (optional)

Chopped fresh parsley for garnish (optional)

Preparation

Prepare the asparagus: In a pot of lightly salted water, bring it to a boil and cook the cut asparagus for 2-3 minutes or until they are tender but still crisp. Drain them and set them aside.

Prepare the Limoncello sauce: In a large pan, melt the butter over medium-low heat. Add the freshly grated ginger and the grated lemon zest and sauté for a minute until they release aromatic fragrances. Pour the Limoncello into the pan with the butter, ginger, and lemon zest. Let it cook for 2-3 minutes, so the alcohol evaporates, and the Limoncello flavor blends with the sauce.

Add the pre-cooked asparagus and the Parmesan cheese: Add the pre-cooked asparagus to the pan with the sauce. Mix well to season them with the Limoncello. Also, add half of the Parmesan cheese and mix until you get a creamy sauce. If the sauce seems too thick, you can add a bit of the pappardelle cooking water to achieve the desired consistency.

Cook and combine the pappardelle: In a large pot, bring a large pot of salted water to a boil. Cook the pappardelle following the package Preparation or until they are al dente. Drain them, but save a small amount of cooking water. Add the pappardelle to the pan with the sauce and gently mix to distribute the sauce evenly over all the pappardelle.

Serve the pappardelle: Transfer the Pappardelle with Limoncello and Asparagus to serving plates. Sprinkle the remaining Parmesan cheese over the pappardelle. If desired, you can garnish with thin slices of fresh ginger, extra grated lemon zest, and chopped fresh parsley.

Serve hot: Serve immediately while it's hot. This dish offers a bold combination of flavors and a unique freshness thanks to the Limoncello and asparagus.

RIGATONI WITH LIMONCELLO, CHERRY TOMATOES, AND BASIL

320gr of rigatoni

200gr of cherry tomatoes

60ml of Limoncello

A bunch of fresh basil

Grated Pecorino cheese

Salt and pepper, to taste

Extra virgin olive oil, as needed

Preparation

In a pan, heat some extra virgin olive oil and add the cherry tomatoes cut in half. Let them cook over medium-high heat until they begin to caramelize slightly. Add the Limoncello to the tomatoes. Be cautious, as it may produce a little flame, so be careful and keep your face away from the pan. Allow the alcohol to evaporate until the flame goes out.

Reduce the heat and add the thinly sliced fresh basil leaves. Mix well to combine the flavors.

Cook the rigatoni in plenty of salted water following the package Preparation until they reach al dente. Drain and add the cooked rigatoni to the pan with the sauce, then gently mix to let them absorb the flavors.

Add grated Pecorino cheese to your liking and mix again.

Serve the Rigatoni with Limoncello, Cherry Tomatoes, and Basil with a sprinkle of freshly ground black pepper and a fresh basil leaf as garnish.

Enjoy this explosion of Mediterranean flavors!

EXCELLENCE MAIN COURSES: LIMONCELLO ON THE TABLE

Welcome to one of the most delectable sections of our culinary journey: the chapter dedicated to main courses prepared with the magical touch of Limoncello. Here, Limoncello marries with top-quality ingredients to create main dishes that are true gastronomic masterpieces. Main courses in Italian cuisine are the epitome of sophistication, and the addition of Limoncello transforms them into extraordinary culinary experiences. From delicate meats to fresh fish, you will discover how Limoncello can bring a new dimension of flavor to each dish. In this section, we will guide you through a series of captivating recipes, each offering a unique perspective on how Limoncello can enrich the palate. From the citrus nuances in Limoncello Fish Fillets to the complexity of Lemon Aromas on an entrecôte, each dish captures the essence of Italian flavor.

Regardless of your culinary expertise, you will find these recipes accessible and rewarding to prepare. Each recipe is accompanied by clear Preparation and readily available ingredients, allowing you to create main courses that will honor your table. Whether you are cooking for a special dinner or looking to enrich your culinary repertoire, these recipes will guide you through an Italian culinary journey that combines tradition and innovation.

LIMONCELLO TUNA

2 fresh tuna fillets

50 ml of Limoncello

Juice of 1 lemon

Grated zest of 1 lemon (only the yellow part)

Salt and black pepper to taste

2 tablespoons of extra virgin olive oil

Fresh chopped parsley for garnish (optional)

Preparation

Start by heating a non-stick skillet over medium-high heat. There's no need to add oil to the pan, as the tuna will release its natural oils during cooking. While the pan is heating, season the tuna fillets with salt and black pepper on both sides. Once the pan is hot, place the tuna fillets in the pan and cook for 1-2 minutes on each side, depending on the thickness of the fillets. The tuna should be pink on the inside to keep it tender and juicy.

Remove the tuna fillets from the pan and set them aside on a plate. In the same pan, pour in the Limoncello and scrape the bottom with a wooden spoon to collect all the juices and flavors from the tuna.

Add the lemon juice and grated lemon zest to the Limoncello. Cook over medium-low heat for about 2-3 minutes, stirring constantly, until the liquid reduces slightly and becomes a light sauce.

Return the tuna fillets to the pan with the Limoncello sauce. Cook for another 1-2 minutes, gently turning the fillets to ensure they are well coated with the fragrant sauce.

Serve the warm Limoncello tuna, garnishing it with a little freshly chopped parsley if desired. This Limoncello Tuna dish will be a delight to the palate, with the fresh and citrusy flavor of Limoncello perfectly complementing the juicy tuna.

LIMONCELLO FISH BRACIOLE

4 fish braciole (swordfish or sea bass work well)

Fresh basil leaves

60 ml of Limoncello

Juice of 1 fresh lemon

Extra virgin olive oil

Salt and freshly ground black pepper

Thin lemon slices (for garnish)

Preparation

To start, prepare the swordfish braciole. Ensure they are well cleaned and pat them dry with paper towels. Remove the skin from the swordfish slices, then cut them into rectangles, keeping the scraps aside. Gently pound them, taking care not to break them.

In a bowl, combine the grated caciocavallo cheese, chopped fish scraps, a little breadcrumbs, chopped basil, and parsley, a drizzle of olive oil, salt, and freshly ground black pepper. Lay the swordfish slices on your work surface, distribute some filling on each slice, and roll them into a roll. Secure them at the end with a toothpick.

In a non-stick skillet, heat some extra virgin olive oil over medium-high heat. When the oil is hot, gently place the basil-wrapped fish braciole in the pan. Cook the fish braciole for a few minutes on each side until they are well browned and the fish is cooked. The cooking time will depend on the thickness of the fish braciole used.

When the fish braciole are almost ready, deglaze the pan with Limoncello. Let it cook for a minute or two to allow the alcohol to evaporate.

Squeeze the juice of a fresh lemon over the braciole in the pan. Season with salt and freshly ground black pepper to taste. Transfer the Limoncello fish braciole to a serving platter. Garnish with thin lemon slices and a few fresh basil leaves.

Serve immediately while the fish braciole are hot and fragrant. You might accompany them with grilled vegetables for a complete meal.

These Limoncello Fish Braciole are a summery delight with a citrusy freshness.

STURGEON STEAKS WITH LIMONCELLO

6 sturgeon steaks with skin

250gr of heavy cream

120gr of black truffle

40gr of shelled pistachios

Lemon zest

Limoncello liqueur

Olive oil

Salt and pepper to taste

Preparation

In a large skillet, heat a drizzle of extra virgin olive oil over medium-high heat. Sear the sturgeon steaks until they are well-browned on both sides. Ensure they are fully cooked. Season the sturgeon steaks with salt and pepper.

Deglaze the steaks with a splash of Limoncello, being careful of any flames. Let it cook until the alcohol has completely evaporated. Add the zest from half a lemon, coarsely chopped pistachios, truffle shavings, and heavy cream to the skillet. Mix well.

Cook for approximately 5-6 minutes, or until the sauce has reduced to a thick syrup that has absorbed all the flavors.

Transfer the sturgeon steaks with the delicious sauce to a serving plate.

STUFFED CALAMARI WITH LIMONCELLO

4 medium-sized calamari

200gr of shrimp or other seafood of your choice

1 cup of breadcrumbs

2 cloves of chopped garlic

Chopped fresh parsley

Salt and freshly ground black pepper

Extra virgin olive oil

Limoncello

Fish or vegetable broth (for cooking)

Lemon juice

Lemon zest

Butter (optional)

Preparation

Begin by cleaning the calamari. Rinse them under running water and gently separate the head from the body, keeping the head aside. Remove the transparent cartilage pen from inside, rinse the squid pouch under running water, and remove the innards with your fingers. Ensure they are cleaned thoroughly. Remove the outer skin by making a small incision at one end with a knife and gently pulling it off. Now, take the head and separate it from the tentacles by cutting just below the eyes. Then, open p the tentacles and push up the central part to remove the beak.

Finely chop the tentacles with a knife. Set the cleaned calamari aside and remove the bread crust and cut the crumb into cubes, then finely chop the parsley after washing it. Heat oil in a skillet, add a clove of garlic and anchovy fillets (you can also add shrimp or other seafood according to your taste), and let them melt gently. Add the chopped tentacles and sauté for 2-3 minutes. Remove the garlic from the pan and add the bread crumbs. After a couple of minutes, deglaze with Limoncello and crush the bread cubes with a spatula or spoon to absorb the dressing well. Once the liquid is absorbed, transfer the mixture to a bowl and let it cool. Then add the grated Parmesan cheese and chopped parsley, a lightly beaten egg, salt, and pepper. Knead the ingredients by hand to compact them well, then transfer the mixture to a pastry bag and cut the tip to a thickness of about 1 cm.

Take the reserved calamari and stuff them with the mixture, being sure to leave a couple of cm from the edge. When all the calamari are stuffed, fold the edges over and close the opening with a toothpick.

In a pan, heat a little oil with a clove of garlic, then place the stuffed calamari inside and cook for a few moments over high heat to seal them. Add a generous splash of Limoncello to the stuffed calamari and let it evaporate for about a minute. This will give a unique flavor to the calamari. As soon as the alcohol has evaporated, add a pinch of salt and cover with a lid. Cook over medium heat for 5-6 minutes, depending on the size of the calamari. When cooking is finished, you can add a knob of butter and lemon juice to create a Limoncello glaze. Stir well until you achieve a creamy consistency.

Serve the stuffed calamari with Limoncello hot, perhaps accompanied by vegetable side dishes.

LIMONCELLO PRAWNS

10 prawns (fresh or frozen)

1 clove of garlic

A drizzle of olive oil

A bunch of chopped parsley

Zest of 1 lemon (grated)

Half a glass of Limoncello

Preparation

In a skillet, drizzle a bit of olive oil and sauté the peeled garlic clove over medium heat. Add the prawns, quickly rinsed under cold running water. Cook the prawns for about a minute in the garlic sauce.

After a minute, remove the garlic clove from the pan. Season the prawns with grated lemon zest and deglaze with Limoncello. Continue cooking the Limoncello prawns until all the alcohol has evaporated.

When cooking is complete, serve the Limoncello prawns hot, with some of the cooking liquid and a sprinkle of chopped parsley for a fresh aromatic touch.

You can also opt for a flambé version: after pouring the Limoncello over the prawns, turn off the stove and ignite the liquid in the pan with a lighter. The flame will extinguish itself once the cooking liquid has completely evaporated.

SCAMPI WITH LIMONCELLO

12-16 scampi (depending on size), cleaned and deveined

2 tablespoons of butter

2 cloves of garlic, finely chopped

60ml of Limoncello

Juice of 1 fresh lemon

2 tablespoons of chopped fresh parsley

Freshly ground black pepper to taste

Lemon slices for garnish

Preparation

In a large non-stick skillet, melt the butter over medium heat. Add the finely chopped garlic cloves and sauté them lightly in the melted butter, being careful not to let them brown or burn.

Add the peeled scampi to the skillet and cook them for 2-3 minutes on one side until they turn pink and opaque. Deglaze the pan with Limoncello by pouring it into the pan. The alcohol will begin to evaporate, creating a delightful aroma.

Squeeze fresh lemon juice over the prawns and mix well. Cook for another 2-3 minutes until the prawns are fully cooked and coated in the Limoncello sauce.

Season the scampi with chopped fresh parsley and freshly ground black pepper to taste. Stir to evenly distribute the seasoning.

Serve the Scampi with Limoncello hot, garnished with lemon slices for a decorative touch. These Scampi with Limoncello are a juicy and flavorful dish, perfect as an appetizer or main course for a special dinner.

LIMONCELLO SALMON

Salmon fillet

Limoncello

Lemon juice

30-60gr of butter

Garlic (1 clove or more to taste)

Chopped fresh parsley

Salt and pepper

Preparation

Start by preparing the Limoncello sauce. In a large skillet, melt a generous amount of butter over medium heat. The amount of butter can vary depending on the size of the salmon fillet and your personal taste, but typically, at least 30-60 grams are used. Add finely chopped garlic to the skillet with the butter and sauté it lightly until it starts to release its fragrant aroma. Make sure not to let it burn, or it could become bitter.

Now, place the salmon fillet in the skillet with the skin side down. Cook the salmon over medium-low heat for a few minutes, turning it gently to ensure even cooking. The cooking time will depend on the thickness of the fillet, but generally, cook the salmon for 3-5 minutes per side until it is tender and opaque in the center.

During the final stages of cooking the salmon, add a generous shot of Limoncello to the skillet. The heat will evaporate the alcohol, leaving behind the delightful lemon aroma. This process should take about 1-2 minutes. You can also add fresh lemon juice to taste to intensify the flavor.

Before serving, sprinkle the salmon with plenty of chopped parsley, salt, and pepper to taste. Fresh parsley will add a touch of freshness and color to the dish.

Transfer the salmon to individual plates and pour the Limoncello sauce over the fish. Serve your Limoncello Salmon hot and enjoy this aromatic and delicious delicacy. This dish is perfect for special occasions or a gourmet dinner at home!

SOLE WITH LIMONCELLO

2 sole fillets

2 tablespoons of butter

2 tablespoons of olive oil

60ml of Limoncello

Juice of 1 fresh lemon

2 tablespoons of capers

Lemon slices for garnish

Salt and pepper to taste

Chopped fresh parsley for decoration (optional)

Preparation

Begin by thoroughly cleaning the sole fillets and pat them dry with paper towels. Make sure to remove any remaining bones.

In a large non-stick skillet, melt the butter in olive oil over medium heat. Be sure not to let the butter burn. Gently place the sole fillets in the skillet with the skin side down. Cook for about 3-4 minutes until the skin side becomes golden and crispy. Carefully flip the fillets and cook the other side for another 2-3 minutes until the fish is evenly cooked and begins to flake.

Deglaze the skillet with Limoncello. You'll notice a pleasant lemon aroma as the Limoncello mixes with the fish juices. Add fresh lemon juice and capers to the skillet. These ingredients will contribute to a fresh and vibrant flavor.

Continue cooking for another minute or two, ensuring that the flavors blend well and the fish is fully cooked. The sole fillets should be tender and easily flaked with a fork.

Taste the dish and adjust the seasoning with salt and pepper according to your personal preferences. To serve, transfer the sole fillets to individual plates and garnish with lemon slices and chopped fresh parsley (if desired).

This dish of Sole with Limoncello is fresh, flavorful, and perfect for an elegant dinner or a special meal. Serve it with vegetable side dishes or rice for a complete meal.

BRANZINO WITH LIMONCELLO

2 whole branzino, cleaned and scaled

Extra virgin olive oil

Salt and freshly ground black pepper to taste

60ml of Limoncello

Juice of 2 fresh lemons

2 tablespoons of sugar

Preparation

Preheat the oven to 180 degrees Celsius (356 degrees Fahrenheit). First, ensure that the branzino have been thoroughly cleaned by removing the innards and scales. Rinse them under running water and pat them dry with paper towels. Make a few shallow cuts on both sides of the branzino. This will help cook them evenly and allow the flavors to penetrate the flesh.

Generously brush olive oil on both sides of the branzino and inside the cavity. Be sure to cover the surface well. Season the branzino generously with salt and pepper, both on the outside and inside. Transfer the branzino to a lightly greased baking dish.

Bake the branzino in the preheated oven for about 20-25 minutes or until the flesh is tender and flakes easily with a fork. The cooking time may vary slightly depending on the size of the fish and the oven temperature, so be careful not to overcook them.

Meanwhile, prepare the Limoncello sauce. In a small saucepan, combine the Limoncello, lemon juice, and sugar. Cook over medium-low heat, stirring continuously until the sugar has completely dissolved, and the sauce has slightly thickened. This should take about 5-7 minutes.

When the branzino are ready, carefully transfer them to a serving platter. Pour the hot Limoncello sauce over the freshly cooked branzino, completely covering them. Serve the Branzino with Limoncello immediately, perhaps garnishing the dish with some fresh lemon slices or a sprinkle of chopped parsley.

This Branzino with Limoncello dish is fresh, aromatic, and perfect for a special dinner. Serve it with vegetable sides or rice for a complete meal. Enjoy your meal!

LIMONCELLO STEAK

1 steak (filet or sirloin) of your choice

Salt and freshly ground black pepper to taste

Extra virgin olive oil

60ml of Limoncello

Fresh herbs like thyme or rosemary (optional)

Preparation

Preheat the grill or a non-stick skillet over medium-high heat. If using a skillet, add a drizzle of olive oil and let it heat up.

While the grill or skillet is heating, prepare the steak. Make sure it's at room temperature by leaving it out of the refrigerator for about 30 minutes before cooking. This will help cook it evenly.

Before cooking the steak, pat it dry with paper towels to remove surface moisture. This will help you get a tastier crust when you cook it.

Lightly brush the steak with olive oil on both sides and season it with salt and freshly ground black pepper to taste. If desired, you can also add fresh herbs like thyme or rosemary for an extra burst of flavor.

Place the steak on the hot grill or in the skillet. Cook it to your desired doneness, turning it only once during cooking. Cooking time will vary depending on the thickness and preferred doneness (rare, medium-rare, medium, etc.).

When the steak is almost ready, deglaze it with Limoncello. Pour the Limoncello over the hot steak and let it evaporate for about 1-2 minutes. This will create a flavorful lemon glaze on the meat.

Remove the steak from the grill or skillet and let it rest for a few minutes before slicing. This will allow the juices to distribute evenly within the meat.

Slice the steak and serve it with the Limoncello glaze on top. You can also add some fresh herbs as garnish, if desired.

Limoncello Steak is a flavorful dish, perfect for meat lovers with a touch of lemony freshness. Serve it with vegetable or potato side dishes for a complete meal. Enjoy your meal!

LIMONCELLO CHICKEN BREAST

650gr of sliced chicken breast

Flour as needed

60gr of butter

1 shot of Limoncello

Juice of 1 lemon

Extra virgin olive oil (EVO) as needed

Salt and pepper to taste

A bunch of parsley

Preparation

Start by squeezing one lemon to obtain fresh lemon juice.

Finely chop the parsley and set it aside.

Coat the chicken breast slices in flour, making sure to shake off the excess.

In a large skillet, melt the butter in a small amount of extra virgin olive oil over medium heat.

Cook the chicken slices in the preheated skillet for about 1 minute per side or until they are well-browned and cooked through. Season with salt and pepper to taste during cooking.

Once the chicken slices are cooked, increase the heat and add the lemon juice and Limoncello. Allow it to cook for a minute or two until the alcohol has completely evaporated, and the sauce has reduced and thickened slightly.

Transfer the Limoncello chicken slices to a serving platter.

Sprinkle the chicken with chopped parsley for a touch of freshness and color.

Serve your delicious Limoncello Chicken Breast immediately, along with its flavorful sauce. Enjoy your meal!

LIMONCELLO ROOSTER

1 small whole rooster (approximately 700-800g)

50 ml of Limoncello

3 cloves of garlic (minced)

Sprigs of fresh rosemary

Freshly ground black pepper

Salt, to taste

Extra virgin olive oil

Preparation

To begin, prepare the marinade for the rooster. In a bowl large enough to hold the rooster, mix together the Limoncello, minced garlic, fresh rosemary (use the leaves and tips of the sprigs), and a generous grind of black pepper. There's no need to add salt at this stage as Limoncello is sweet enough.

Prepare the rooster by removing any innards and washing it thoroughly under running water. Pat it dry with care using paper towels.

Place the rooster in the marinade, making sure it is fully coated with all the flavors. Cover the bowl with plastic wrap and refrigerate for at least 2-4 hours, or overnight if possible, to allow the rooster to absorb all the flavors.

After marinating, preheat the oven to 180°C (356°F) or prepare an outdoor grill for cooking.

If you'd like to bake the rooster, transfer it to a lightly oiled baking dish. Sprinkle a little extra salt and additional pepper on top of the rooster if desired.

Bake the rooster in the preheated oven for approximately 45-60 minutes or until the skin is golden and crispy, and the meat is cooked.

If you prefer to grill the rooster, heat the grill to medium-high heat. Place the rooster on the grill and turn it occasionally, basting it with the remaining marinade, until it is well-cooked and nicely browned. This should take around 30-40 minutes depending on the rooster's size and grill temperature.

Once cooked, serve the hot Limoncello Rooster, perhaps with a squeeze of fresh lemon juice and a couple of fresh rosemary sprigs as garnish.

This Limoncello Rooster will be a delight with its fresh and aromatic flavor. Enjoy your meal!

LIMONCELLO PORK

1 pork roast (approximately 1.5 kg)

60 ml of Limoncello

3 tablespoons of sugar

Juice of 2 fresh lemons

Grated zest of 2 lemons

Salt and freshly ground black pepper

Extra virgin olive oil

Fresh rosemary (for garnish)

Preparation

Preheat the oven to 180°C (356°F).

In a bowl, prepare a marinade by mixing the fresh lemon juice, grated lemon zest, Limoncello, a pinch of salt, and freshly ground black pepper. This marinade will give the pork a fresh and citrusy flavor.

Massage the pork roast with the marinade evenly, making sure it is completely covered. Allow the pork to marinate for at least 30 minutes at room temperature, or you can refrigerate it for several hours or overnight for a more intense flavor.

In a flameproof skillet, heat some extra virgin olive oil over medium-high heat. When the oil is hot, add the pork roast to the skillet and sear it on all sides until it's well-browned. This step will seal the juices inside the meat.

Transfer the pork roast to a roasting pan. Add fresh rosemary on top of the roast for an aromatic touch.

Roast the pork in the preheated oven for about 1.5-2 hours or until the meat reaches an internal temperature of 70-75°C (160-170°F). You can check the temperature with a meat thermometer inserted into the thickest part of the roast.

Meanwhile, prepare the Limoncello glaze. In a small saucepan, melt the sugar over medium heat. Once the sugar has completely melted and starts to turn golden, add the Limoncello and cook for a couple of minutes until the sauce slightly thickens.

Once the pork roast is cooked, remove it from the oven and let it rest for about 10 minutes before slicing.

Before serving, drizzle the Limoncello glaze over the pork slices. This glaze will give the pork a unique and delightful flavor.

Serve the hot Limoncello Pork, perhaps with vegetable or roasted potato sides. Enjoy your meal!

LIMONCELLO DESSERTS: A TOUCH OF SWEETNESS FROM THE AMALFI COAST

Welcome to the section of Limoncello-based desserts, a realm of sweet delights that blend the best of Neapolitan tradition with the magical touch of Italy's most beloved citrus fruit. In this paragraph, we will explore a series of desserts that will transform every meal into an unforgettable experience. Desserts are the culmination of every Italian meal, a palate-pleasing celebration that marks the end of a meal with taste and refinement. With the addition of Limoncello, these desserts become culinary works of art. Here, you will find a wide range of irresistible sweets, from cakes to creams, from ice creams to cookies, all crafted with the unmistakable aroma of Limoncello. Each recipe is a celebration of Italian flavors and traditions, designed to delight your senses and satisfy your sweet tooth. From the zesty and refreshing notes of Limoncello Panna Cotta to the irresistible temptation of Limoncello Tiramisu, these recipes will take you on a culinary journey through the world of Italian desserts with a citrusy twist.

Whether you're an aspiring pastry chef or simply a lover of sweets, you'll find these recipes accessible and enjoyable to prepare. Each recipe will be accompanied by detailed Preparation and easily accessible ingredients, making the creation process a sweet and fulfilling experience. Get ready to immerse yourself in a world of sweetness and conclude every meal with a touch of refinement and satisfaction. So, prepare to satisfy your craving for sweet Italian dreams with Limoncello!

LIMONCELLO TIRAMISÙ

250gr mascarpone

3 eggs

100gr sugar

200ml Limoncello

200ml cooled coffee

200gr ladyfingers

Zest of 2 lemons

Icing sugar for decoration

Preparation

Prepare the coffee and let it cool. Add Limoncello to the cooled coffee.

Separate the egg yolks from the egg whites. In a bowl, whisk the egg yolks with sugar until you get a clear and creamy mixture.

Add the mascarpone to the sugared egg yolks and mix well until you get a smooth cream.

Whip the egg whites to stiff peaks in another bowl.

Gently fold the whipped egg whites into the mascarpone and egg yolk cream. Mix with gentle, upward strokes to maintain the fluffy texture.

In an oven dish or individual serving dishes, start assembling the Tiramisù. Quickly dip each ladyfinger into the Limoncello coffee and place it on the bottom of the dish.

Cover the ladyfingers with a layer of mascarpone cream and sprinkle a generous amount of grated lemon zest.

Repeat the process, creating alternating layers of ladyfingers and cream until you've used up all the ingredients. The final layer should be cream.

Cover the dish or individual dishes with plastic wrap and refrigerate for at least 4 hours, preferably overnight, so the Tiramisù can firm up and the flavors meld.

Before serving, dust the Tiramisù's surface with icing sugar and decorate with thin lemon slices or grated lemon zest.

Your Limoncello Tiramisù is ready to enjoy! It's a fresh and aromatic dessert, perfect for special occasions or just to treat yourself to a refined sweet.

LIMONCELLO PANNA COTTA

500ml fresh cream

100ml Limoncello

100gr sugar

2 gelatin sheets

Zest of 2 lemons

Thin lemon slices for decoration (optional)

Preparation

Place the gelatin sheets in cold water to soften them. In a saucepan, pour the cream and sugar. Heat them over medium heat, stirring constantly until the sugar is completely dissolved. Do not bring the cream to a boil; it should be warm but not boiling.

Remove the saucepan from the heat and add the softened gelatin. Stir well until the gelatin is completely dissolved in the warm cream.

Add the Limoncello and grated lemon zest to the mixture. Continue to stir to ensure all the ingredients are well combined.

Pour the mixture into molds or individual cups. Cover with plastic wrap and refrigerate for at least 4 hours, preferably overnight, to allow the panna cotta to set.

Before serving, decorate with thin lemon slices or grated lemon zest, if desired.

Your Limoncello Panna Cotta is ready to be enjoyed! This creamy and refreshing dessert is ideal for finishing a summer meal or indulging in a touch of lemony delight.

LIMONCELLO SOUFFLÉ

3 eggs (separated yolks and whites)

1/2 cup of sugar

2 tablespoons of flour

1/4 cup of Limoncello

1/4 cup of fresh lemon juice

Zest of 2 lemons

Butter and sugar for the ramekins

Icing sugar for dusting (optional)

Preparation

Preheat the oven to 180°C (350°F). Butter and sugar the soufflé ramekins.

In a bowl, beat the egg yolks with sugar until you have a fluffy and light-colored mixture.

Add the sifted flour and mix well until you have a homogeneous mixture.

Add the Limoncello, lemon juice, and grated lemon zest to the yolk mixture. Mix well.

In another bowl, whip the egg whites to stiff peaks using an electric whisk or mixer.

Gently fold the whipped egg whites into the yolk and lemon mixture. Mix with gentle, upward movements to avoid deflating the egg whites.

Pour the mixture into the prepared ramekins, filling them about three-quarters full.

Bake in the preheated oven for approximately 15-20 minutes or until the soufflés are golden on top and puffed. Do not open the oven during baking to prevent the soufflés from collapsing.

Once ready, remove the soufflés from the oven and dust with icing sugar, if desired.

Serve immediately as soufflés tend to deflate quickly.

Your Limoncello Soufflé is ready to be enjoyed. This light and fragrant dessert will be an excellent conclusion to a special meal.

LIMONCELLO TART

250gr of all-purpose flour

100gr of cold, cubed butter

100gr of powdered sugar

1 egg

Zest of 1 lemon

A pinch of salt

Ingredients for the Limoncello Filling:

3 egg yolks

150ml of Limoncello

100gr of sugar

50gr of butter

Juice of 2 lemons

Zest of 2 lemons

2 tablespoons of cornstarch (cornflour)

Preparation

Shortcrust Pastry Preparation: In a bowl, sift the flour and combine it with the cold, cubed butter. Work the mixture quickly with your hands until it resembles a sandy texture.

Add the powdered sugar, grated lemon zest, the egg, and a pinch of salt. Work the dough quickly until it forms a compact ball. Wrap it in plastic wrap and refrigerate it for at least 30 minutes.

Limoncello Filling Preparation: In a saucepan, mix the egg yolks, sugar, and cornstarch to obtain a homogeneous mixture.

Add the Limoncello, lemon juice, and grated lemon zest to the mixture. Mix well.

Place the saucepan over low heat and add the butter. Heat and stir constantly until the cream thickens. This will take about 5-7 minutes. Set aside.

Assembly and Baking: Preheat the oven to 180°C (350°F).

Remove the tart dough from the refrigerator and roll it out on a lightly floured surface to create a large circle large enough to line a 22-24cm diameter tart pan.

Poke the bottom of the pastry with a fork and pour the Limoncello filling inside.

You can decorate the surface with strips of pastry if you prefer a lattice design or leave it smooth.

Bake the tart in the preheated oven for about 25-30 minutes or until the surface is golden.

Once baked, allow it to cool completely before serving.

Your Limoncello Tart is ready to be enjoyed. This dessert is a delightful combination of crunchiness and creaminess with an incredible lemon aroma. Enjoy!

LIMONCELLO SEMIFREDDO

4 egg yolks

150gr sugar

Zest of 2 untreated lemons

Juice of 4 lemons

100ml Limoncello

400ml fresh cream

4 egg whites

50gr powdered sugar

Dry cookies (like ladyfingers) for decoration (optional)

Preparation

Limoncello Mixture Preparation: In a bowl, mix the egg yolks with 150gr of sugar until you get a foamy and light mixture. Add the grated lemon zest and lemon juice to the mixture. Mix well. Gradually incorporate the Limoncello into the mixture while continuing to stir.

Cream Mixture Preparation: In a separate bowl, whip the fresh cream until you get soft peaks. Make sure the cream is cold. In another bowl, whip the egg whites to stiff peaks. Gradually add 50gr of powdered sugar while continuing to whip until you get stiff peaks.

Gently fold the whipped cream mixture into the Limoncello mixture. Then, with gentle, upward movements, also fold in the whipped egg whites. This will give your semifreddo a soft and light texture.

Semifreddo Assembly: Prepare a loaf pan by lining it with plastic wrap for easy unmolding later. Pour the semifreddo mixture into the prepared pan. If you like, you can add a layer of dry cookies (like ladyfingers) on the surface of the semifreddo for an extra crunchy touch.

Cover the pan with plastic wrap and place the semifreddo in the freezer for at least 6 hours, or preferably overnight.

Serving: Before serving, unmold the Limoncello semifreddo onto a serving platter. You can decorate the semifreddo with thin lemon slices

LIMONCELLO CUPCAKES

Ingredients for the Cupcakes:

1 1/2 cups of cake flour

1 1/2 teaspoons of baking powder

1/4 teaspoon of baking soda

A pinch of salt

1/2 cup of softened butter

1 cup of sugar

2 eggs

2 tablespoons of grated lemon zest

2 tablespoons of Limoncello

1/2 cup of whole milk

Ingredients for the Limoncello Frosting:

1/2 cup of softened butter

4 cups of powdered sugar

2 tablespoons of Limoncello

Zest of 1 lemon

2-3 tablespoons of lemon juice

Thin lemon slices or grated lemon zest for decoration (optional)

Preparation

Cupcakes Preparation: Preheat the oven to 180°C (350°F) and prepare a muffin tray with paper liners. In a medium bowl, sift the flour, baking powder, baking soda, and salt. Mix well and set aside.

In another bowl, using an electric mixer, beat the butter until creamy. Gradually add the sugar and continue beating until the mixture becomes light and fluffy.

Add the eggs one at a time, making sure to fully incorporate each one before adding the next.

Add the grated lemon zest and Limoncello to the butter and egg mixture. Mix well.

Alternately, fold the dry ingredient mixture and the milk into the wet mixture, starting and ending with the dry ingredients. Mix only until the ingredients are combined, being careful not to overmix and weigh down the cupcake batter.

Distribute the batter evenly among the paper liners in the muffin tray.

Bake the cupcakes in the preheated oven for about 18-20 minutes or until a toothpick inserted into the center comes out clean.

Remove the cupcakes from the tray and let them cool completely on a wire rack.

Limoncello Frosting Preparation: Using an electric mixer, beat the softened butter until creamy.

Gradually add the powdered sugar, continuing to beat until you achieve a smooth frosting.

Add the Limoncello, lemon zest, and lemon juice to the frosting. Continue to beat until you reach a spreadable consistency.

Assembly: When the cupcakes are completely cooled, generously spread the Limoncello frosting on top of each cupcake.

If desired, decorate with thin lemon slices or grated lemon zest for a fresh and colorful touch.

Serve and enjoy your delicious Limoncello Cupcakes! These cupcakes are perfect for any occasion, from parties to after-dinner desserts. The Limoncello adds a touch of freshness and citrus flavor that makes them irresistible. Enjoy!

LIMONCELLO ICE CREAM

2 cups of heavy cream

1 cup of whole milk

1 cup of sugar

1/2 cup of Limoncello

Zest of 2 untreated lemons

Juice of 2 lemons

A pinch of salt

Preparation

In a bowl, whisk together the milk and sugar until the sugar is completely dissolved.

Add the heavy cream and mix well.

Add the Limoncello and mix until you have a homogeneous mixture.

Add the grated lemon zest and lemon juice to the mixture. Be sure not to add the lemon seeds.

Add a pinch of salt to enhance the flavors.

Pour the mixture into your ice cream maker and proceed with making the ice cream following the manufacturer's Preparation.

If you don't have an ice cream maker, you can pour the mixture into an airtight container and place it in the freezer. Every 30-45 minutes, vigorously stir the ice cream with a spoon to prevent ice crystals from forming. Repeat this process for at least 3-4 hours or until the ice cream is well solidified.

Once the ice cream is ready, transfer it to an airtight container and store it in the freezer until serving.

Before serving, you can decorate the Limoncello ice cream with a sprinkle of grated lemon zest or a thin lemon slice for a fresh and appealing touch.

Serve the Limoncello ice cream in bowls or cones and enjoy this delightful lemony sweetness with a touch of Limoncello! Limoncello ice cream is perfect for a hot summer day or as a dessert after a meal. The fresh and lively lemon flavor with the hint of bitter Limoncello makes it an irresistible summer dessert. Enjoy!

LIMONCELLO CHEESECAKE:

Ingredients for the Crust:

200gr digestive biscuits or graham crackers

100gr melted butter

Ingredients for the Filling:

500gr cream cheese (Philadelphia-style)

200gr sugar

3 eggs

250ml heavy cream

60ml Limoncello

Zest of 2 untreated lemons

2 tablespoons of flour

A pinch of salt

Ingredients for the Topping:

200ml heavy cream

2 tablespoons powdered sugar

30ml Limoncello

Thin lemon slices for decoration (optional)

Preparation

Preheat the oven to 160°C (320°F). Line the bottom of a 23cm cheesecake pan with parchment paper.

To prepare the crust, pulse the digestive biscuits in a food processor until they have a crumb-like texture. Add the melted butter and mix until it's a moist mixture. Press this mixture into the bottom of the pan and refrigerate while you prepare the filling.

In a large bowl, beat the cream cheese with the sugar until you have a smooth mixture.

Add the eggs one at a time, ensuring each is fully incorporated before adding the next.

Add the heavy cream, Limoncello, lemon zest, flour, and a pinch of salt to the mixture. Mix well until you have a homogeneous mixture.

Pour the mixture over the biscuit base in the pan and level it.

Bake in the preheated oven for approximately 45-50 minutes or until the center is just jiggly but not liquid.

Remove the cheesecake from the oven and let it cool to room temperature. Then transfer it to the refrigerator and let it cool for at least 4 hours, preferably overnight.

To prepare the topping, whip the heavy cream with powdered sugar until soft peaks form. Add the Limoncello and gently fold it in.

When you are ready to serve, remove the cheesecake from the pan and decorate it with the Limoncello whipped cream. If desired, add some thin lemon slices as decoration.

Slice and serve your delicious Limoncello cheesecake. Enjoy! This Limoncello cheesecake is perfect for those who love the fresh and citrusy taste of lemon with a touch of sweetness from the Limoncello. It's an elegant dessert that will delight your guests on any special occasion.

LIMONCELLO SORBET:

500ml water

250g sugar

250ml Limoncello

Fresh juice of 4-5 untreated lemons

Zest of 1 untreated lemon

Preparation

In a saucepan, bring the water and sugar to a boil, stirring until the sugar has completely dissolved. Let it boil for 2-3 minutes to create a light syrup. Remove from heat and let it cool completely.

Once cooled, add the Limoncello, fresh lemon juice, and lemon zest to the syrup. Mix well to combine all the ingredients.

Transfer the mixture to an ice cream maker and start the freezing process following the manufacturer's Preparation. If you don't have an ice cream maker, you can also pour the mixture into a freezer-proof container and place it in the freezer, stirring it every 30-45 minutes with a fork until the sorbet is completely frozen and has a smooth consistency.

After freezing the sorbet, transfer it to an airtight container and store it in the freezer until serving.

Before serving, you can decorate the sorbet with a few fresh lemon slices or a sprig of mint if desired.

Enjoy your Limoncello sorbet as a fresh and refreshing dessert after a summer meal or whenever you crave something sweet and citrusy.

This Limoncello sorbet is perfect for refreshing your palate on hot summer days. Its vibrant and aromatic flavor makes it an ideal dessert for those who love the fresh taste of lemons and the slightly bitter touch of Limoncello.

CONCLUSIONS

Limoncello is much more than just a liqueur. It is a symbol of tradition, passion, and the love for good Italian cuisine. In this journey through the history, production, and culture of Limoncello, we have discovered how deeply rooted this liqueur is in Italy's history and soul.

From the picturesque hills of the Amalfi Coast and the Sorrento Peninsula to the tables of Italian families, Limoncello has found its place as a culinary and cultural treasure. We have explored the uncertain origins of this beverage, from legends of monks crafting the liquor in monasteries to stories of ancient family traditions.

We have learned how lemons abound in Italy and are an integral part of the country's agriculture and cuisine, with Limoncello serving as their global ambassador. Their unique flavor and aromatic essential oils contribute to creating a liquor that has become a true Italian icon.

You have discovered how to make Limoncello at home, following the simple yet essential steps of this craft. Now you can experience the authentic taste of Italian lemons wherever you are.

Finally, we have heard stories and anecdotes from those who have a special connection with Limoncello. From families producing it for generations to travelers bringing Limoncello as a precious souvenir, these stories demonstrate that Limoncello is more than just a beverage; it is a bond between people and their experiences.

Limoncello is an expression of Italian hospitality, a celebration of life, and a culinary art. We hope this book has inspired you to further explore the world of Limoncello and to appreciate the beauty of one of Italy's greatest delights. After all, Limoncello is like a friendly smile, a small gesture that can bring joy to anyone who tastes it. To your health and to Limoncello, a treasure of Italy to be shared with the world..

Made in the USA
Las Vegas, NV
13 December 2023